The Man of Passage

The Man of Passage

Ian Mathie

LIVE WIRE

First published in 2006 by
Live Wire Books
The Orchard, School Lane
Warmington, Banbury
Oxfordshire OX17 1DE

Telephone: 01295 690624
Email: info@livewirebooks.com
www.livewirebooks.com

ISBN 0-9553124-1-8 / 978-0-9553124-1-0

Designed by Dick Malt
Cover photograph and line drawings by Ian Mathie

A catalogue record for this book is available from
The British Library.

Further copies of this book are available from:
GTPR Ltd
1 Dog Lane, Fenny Compton
Southam CV47 2YD

Telephone: 01295 770207
Fax: 01295 770202
Email: books@gtpr.com

Contents

For my Mum and Dad, who opened the first door
and encouraged me to walk through.

Introduction

Africa is a continent of profound and startling contrasts. It has many peoples, many languages and many cultures, exhibiting such a colourful diversity that an outsider's interest cannot help but be attracted. To most western minds, Africa is a mysterious place where primitive beliefs uphold barbarous practices and civilisation is no more than a transient veneer. This is far from true, but it is necessary to live with Africa and absorb it into one's soul before it is possible truly to appreciate the richness and variety of what it has to offer.

My own introduction to Africa came at the age of four, when my soldier father was posted to what was then Northern Rhodesia, now Zambia. There were no jet airliners in those days. Our family first travelled by sea to Capetown and the two-week voyage was then followed by a spectacular but exhausting four-day-long rail journey all the way up to Lusaka. There I was sent to my first school, a convent located a few miles outside town that was run by a mixed group of German and Italian nuns.

At first, I was the only white child among two hundred or so African youngsters. Later, five or six other white children came to the school. I was part of an ethnic minority and didn't realise it. None of us did – and none of us would have cared, anyway; we were all just kids together.

Most of the teaching was done in the local languages. English was taught as a foreign language – and then only to the older students. Out of school, I spent much more time playing with our cook's children and my other African friends than I did with the other white army brats, and I saw nothing odd in this.

I often stayed in their homes, shared their food and was cuddled by their mothers if I fell and hurt myself. In every way, I was accepted as one of their own. They were treated the same when they came to our house.

Years later, when I joined the RAF, I met up again with one of the boys who had been to that school with me. He had gone on to join the Zambian Air Force and was sent to Britain for training. We were on the same course, but did not at first recognise one another. One evening in the bar the subject somehow got round to school transport and I was recounting an incident that had taken place on the school bus all those years before. As I paused to take a sip of beer, a rich chocolate voice from just behind me took over the story and the hair on my neck stood up. Gilbert had been on the same bus that day, had witnessed the same events, and recalled them just as clearly. The years fell away, bits of now unfamiliar language came back, and friendship was the same after a twelve-year gap as it had been before.

Soldiers get posted and our family eventually moved on to the Far East. However, we landed again in Africa a few years later. This time it was West Africa, with different peoples, different languages, new cultures and independence in its infancy. By now, I had been sent to a boarding school in England. I hated the regimented, almost monastic existence, with all its restrictions and people with whom I felt I had very little in common. I didn't understand them or share their values and interests. I didn't fit in and didn't want to.

School holidays meant freedom, and I was lucky enough to spend most of the Christmas, Easter and summer vacations back in Africa. I soon made new friends and started acquiring a smattering of new languages. Everything was new and yet, at the same time, it was also familiar, normal and comfortable. Much of my time there was spent visiting the markets with my local friends, catching strange fish in the nearby rivers or wandering around the bush villages absorbing the culture; and also, as we got older and took an interest in such things, drinking the local millet beer.

One summer, in Nigeria, we all went to a district agricultural fair and I was persuaded by my friends to take part in the goat skinning competition. This was a noisy and somewhat gory activity which, much to everyone's amazement – not least my own – I won. I received ten pounds from the local Emir as my prize. He took most of it back off me later when I bought a horse from him for eight pounds, complete with native tack and saddle.

Returning to school was like going back to prison and I tended to adopt solo sports and other activities that I could pursue by myself simply in order to retain some element of my own individuality. It may seem surprising after this that I volunteered for the RAF, but by then my heart was set on flying. A career as an RAF pilot wasn't to be; the government of the day decided on a series of defence cuts and, finding myself stuck on the ground with no prospect of further airborne service, I resigned my commission.

Africa soon drew me again and before long I was back, working this time on development aid projects. I started out in West Africa, based on the coast at Lomé but regularly driving northwards a thousand kilometres or so to the arid sub-Saharan territories I was to come to know so well.

Over the next few years, my work took me all over the continent. And for much of the time it involved living and working among isolated communities, where tribal traditions were strong and contacts with the developed world were very limited, if they existed at all.

For the people in these communities, life is lived from day to day. Their immediate needs are all that matters. The past has little practical use and is often retained in memory more as a curiosity than a justification of how things came to be as they are now, or as a benchmark for the future. The future is frequently a tenuous concept that reaches little further ahead than the next few days. Even in those places where people's survival is less precarious, most find little incentive to look beyond the temporal horizon and prefer to occupy themselves with the affairs of the present. To do otherwise would be seen as deviant; it would awaken a host of taboos, superstitions and deeply rooted cultural imperatives.

Living as intimately as I did in rural villages, one soon falls into a pattern of acceptance, observing the same customs as one's hosts. Not only does this make one more readily acceptable, it also opens doorways that would otherwise remain irrevocably closed, making it possible to blend in and become part of the community. Only then can one begin to understand and appreciate the richness and diversity of the people, their lives and culture.

Western people frequently have difficulty understanding the principles on which such traditions are based, simply because they tend to be analytical and descriptive in their approach. They need to rationalise, to explain the how and why, and everything becomes an intellectual abstraction. Africans allow themselves to feel things as they are.

Living alone among them and becoming actively involved in their everyday existence helped to open that doorway of feeling for me. Even so, with a western education and the influence of western attitudes, I was as capable as any raw outsider of sometimes misunderstanding and often had to be corrected and put in my place by those who knew better – my hosts.

In a village in Upper Volta – now known as Burkina Faso – where I had been sent to initiate a development project, an old man, who had never been to school and could neither read nor write, interrupted my explanation of the project and asked me why I had been born with two ears and only one voice. "Our people know what they need and what they want," he said. "Listen to us and we will tell you. Then, and only then, is it possible that all your educated knowledge may be of some use to us."

He was right, of course, and fortunately I had the sense to recognise this and listen. He and many others like him taught me so much and in time, perhaps, some of my knowledge did become useful. Certainly, I have the small satisfaction of knowing that the results of some of my efforts are still in use.

It is terribly tempting, with the burden of a Western education, to assume that we can improve on what is already there; that we know better. But Africa's people have lived with their environment since the dawn of humanity. They are attuned to their environment and understand it in a way that western man ignored and forgot when he first started developing technology. All too easily, we see the contrasts that Africa offers as being negative and contradictory. This has been the source of the many misunderstandings that have both caused and fuelled so many of Africa's problems.

Although frequently working among illiterate people in situations where taking notes might easily lead to suspicion, I did manage to keep a series of journals whilst living in Africa. The incidents recounted in the following pages are all extracted from those journals. In telling these stories I have tried to give them life and feeling without undue embellishment; they do not need it.

As I say, Africa is a continent of contrasts where the unusual is commonplace and anything can happen. Much has changed since these incidents took place, yet the essence of the environment in which they occurred remains essentially the same.

I encountered **The Man of Passage** in the Danakil desert in Ethiopia. Located at the northern end of the Great Rift Valley, three hundred feet below sea level, this is the region where the fossilised remains of man's earliest ancestors are only now being uncovered, revealing it as the likely cradle of the human race. Today, however, the environment there is as harsh and inhospitable as you will find anywhere on Earth, midday temperatures often reaching over one hundred and forty five degrees Fahrenheit. If it were not so dry it would be unbearable. The drought in the early 1970's decimated the population and wiped out over three quarters of their livestock.

The Visa, although it was obtained in London, gives some of the flavour of bureaucracy in Africa. The Ghanaians are lovely people and their bureaucracy is actually less onerous and inhibiting than most.

Sankarani lies in the far west of Mali, not far from the borders of Senegal and Guinea, near where the mighty Niger River is born. It is a thinly populated area, difficult to get to, and seldom visited by outsiders.

Although **Sphinx** is recounted in the third person, this was simply in order to reduce the number of 'I's in the text. It was, in fact, a very personal experience. The setting is, again, the Danakil desert region of Ethiopia.

Togo Telephone Tango happened, naturally enough, in Togo. The capital, Lomé, is a charming little town on the coast, jammed up against the border with Ghana and backed by a very smelly, mosquito infested lagoon with an escarpment behind. The city has now spread up onto the higher ground, an area that is composed mainly of housing developments; the working heart of the city is on the low ground between the escarpment and the sea.

Bones of Contention is from Upper Volta (or Burkina Faso as it is now called). In a small village some hundred and twenty kilometres north-west of the capital, Ouagadougou, I rebuilt a derelict house and settled in. To work my field, I trained a donkey to the plough, planted new crops and made friends with the villagers and their dogs. Life in the village was never dull!

Arnie's Wives live in an inaccessible, forested part of south-western Togo. The community has little need of the outside world, but occasionally something happens that means they have to become involved. They are not in any respect secretive or reclusive by nature, they just don't often need anyone else.

The Missionary's Feet were firmly planted in the delta of the Niger River in south-eastern Nigeria. Sadly, Robert Sinclair's wife – I never knew her first name – caught cholera and died three years after moving out to Africa. Her husband stayed on and later moved to another mission in Cameroun.

San Prison Blues comes from Mali. The town of San is an outpost on the edge of what used to be a huge area of swamp that borders the River Niger. Unfortunately, much of it has now dried out. My troubles in San grew out of my failure to make a courtesy call on the local Governor when I first arrived in the town.

A Short Walk in Ituri took me from western Uganda through the north eastern corner of Zaïre, (now called the Democratic Republic of Congo). A chance encounter in Entebbe with a group of Canadians who were going trekking in the Ruwenzori Mountains provided me with the opportunity to realise two long held ambitions – to visit the fabled Mountains of the Moon and to go into the Ituri forest and meet the BaMbuti Pygmies.

The Headman's Dilemmas came about in northern Cameroun, in a mountainous region where the remote communities have little contact with the outside world, and even less need of it. The people's traditions and taboos have very deep roots and, whilst visitors are made welcome, most outsiders are viewed with suspicion until their value to the community has been demonstrated.

Anélouha's Secret revealed itself in eastern Ivory Coast, where I worked with her husband, Mbaloé, on water projects to support his vegetable growing and nutrition outreach programmes.

The **Footprints in the Dust** were left in northern Nigeria, soon after independence. In the company of local boys my own age, I spent a great deal of time roaming the bush, although not always with as much excitement as this trip provided.

The **Hippopotamus Hiatus** took place in the deep forest of Zaïre (now the Democratic Republic of Congo). Rivers are plentiful in this steamy jungle region, as are all those creatures, great and small, that love a watery home. The forest people generally live in harmony with their wildlife neighbours, but sometimes someone breaks the rules.

Immigration Control in Togo took a new form when I arrived by air wearing my kilt. This made such a deep and lasting impression on the officials that they never let me forget it.

The Girl Named Ian was christened in Upper Volta (now Burkina Faso), when I made a flying visit to an isolated mission station.

I have been fortunate to have travelled widely and to have met many fascinating and hospitable people. Wherever I went I was welcomed, lodged and fed. My needs were provided for and my soul was nourished. Perhaps I, too, have been a man of passage; less destitute, but more burdened by responsibilities and opportunities than the man who first held that title.

The Man of Passage

We had been surveying down beyond the Chelaka for five days when the man suddenly appeared. The job had been going well and we were almost finished. Two more days would see the whole project completed.

We were sitting in the shade of an enormous acacia tree, discussing the results of the morning's activities. The lone acacia was the only tree on our side of the river, where the land was otherwise covered by dense thorn scrub, interspersed with patches of sparse, dry grass. The survey had actually been made more difficult because it was almost impossible to see more than about forty yards through the scrub. As a result, frequent movements of the theodolite had been necessary and this had wasted a considerable amount of time.

We had pitched our tent close to the edge of the river bank, beneath the sweeping boughs of the huge tree. Being more or less in the open, the camp had not so far become a target for the troop of olive baboons that had taken up residence below the bend on the other side of the river.

To describe it as a river was really too generous. There was almost no flow in the unnamed stream and the level was low enough for the baboons to cross with ease and without getting unduly wet. So far, they had left us alone, although we often heard them barking, particularly at dawn.

The heat haze was always bad during the midday hours, so we normally stopped work from noon until around three and sat in our patch of shade after lunch to do the paperwork. While my two colleagues calculated their theodolite readings and transferred the levels and angles to the plan, I sorted through the morning's collection of samples, made some preliminary tests and recorded the results in my book, cross-referencing with the plan so as to identify the locations from which the samples had been taken.

The series of tests having been completed, I was just packing up the box of reagents, which would not be needed again, when the man suddenly materialised, seemingly out of nowhere.

Emerging from the surrounding scrub, he walked very slowly and deliberately around our little camp, finally stopping in front of the open tent flap. Unhurriedly, he then squatted down on his heels just outside the dense shade of the tree, next to a leafless thorn bush. He was an old man, the oldest any of us had yet seen in that forsaken land where everything was shrivelled by drought and burned up by the sun. Normal life expectancy there was little more than thirty-five, but this desiccated creature must have been nearer sixty-five. Almost completely bald, with just a grey friar's fringe at the back of his head, he had a wispy white beard that had been carefully clipped. He was thin to the point of emaciation and the skin hung in loose wrinkles over his spindly limbs.

He remained squatting, in silence, with his eyes screwed up against the sun, watching and examining us minutely. His bony left hand rested on his knee, the gnarled forefinger hooked loosely through the handle of a battered, soot-encrusted, aluminium kettle. His right hand held firmly onto a short forked stick that he had been carrying over his shoulders and which now served to steady him in his pose.

"Hello," we said.

The man remained immobile, staring at the three of us in turn, as if trying to decide whether or not we were fit to be spoken to. When he eventually made up his mind and spoke, it was with a voice that was as old as time and as desiccated as the desert which surrounded us.

"You have come here," he said.

"Yes," Mohamed answered. "We came five days before."

The old man said nothing, but continued his careful scrutiny.

We had just brewed some tea and, without asking, Mohamed ladled sugar into a glassful and held it out towards the visitor. The old man looked at it for a moment then set down his kettle, transferred the stick to his left hand and, with a slight nod, accepted the glass.

I was intrigued by the way in which this solitary wanderer

remained so silent. We often received visits from the nomads who lived in this region and we had become familiar with what was a ritual form of greeting. This was normally a garrulous process that could last for anything up to twenty minutes. First, it involved detailed enquiries about the wellbeing of one's father, mother, grandparents, brothers, children, livestock and the world and his wife in general before moving on to any news or gossip one might have picked up about such matters as the state of grazing in the area. Only when all these topics had been exhausted would one get down to talking business or discussing other more important subjects, such as raids by other tribes. This wordy and long drawn-out form of introduction is common right across Africa, designed to give strangers the opportunity to weigh each other up. And yet this old man had been squatting there for at least a quarter of an hour and in all that time had uttered only four words.

I looked at him again. He wore the usual rough cotton *gaabi* draped over his scrawny shoulders, with a piece of similar cloth round his waist. On his feet he had a pair of crude sandals made from untanned goat skin. Apart from the kettle and his hand-worn stick, he appeared to have no other possessions.

The old man continued to watch us for a long time, slurping noisily at the scalding tea.

"Do you want to buy a camel?" he eventually asked without any preamble.

I shook my head and looked inquiringly at the other two.

"Want a camel, Mo?" I asked. Mohamed shook his head. "Yusuf?" He, too, shook his head.

Mohamed then turned to the old man. "Thank you, but we have no need of a camel."

The old man seemed unmoved and unsurprised, and said nothing. We looked around for the subject of the proposed deal, but there was no sign of any camel.

Mohamed gave the man some more tea. He accepted it in silence, with only the same slight nod of thanks as before, and proceeded to suck noisily at the sweet, sticky brew. He continued to watch us with his rheumy old eyes, but said nothing more.

A baboon barked on the far side of the river. The yellow weaver birds chattered raucously in the canopy above us as they fluttered about, adding grass to the globular nests that hung precariously from the tips of the thorny branches. These were the only sounds as the world around us dozed through the midday heat.

The old man finished his tea and placed the empty glass on its side in the dust beside him. Transferring the stick to his right hand, he hooked a finger through the handle of his kettle, resumed his former position, and continued to watch us in silence.

After a while he stood up, turned on his heel and, at the same unhurried pace at which he had arrived, walked off into the scrub, without a word of either thanks or farewell.

"Do you want some tea?" I called after him and picked up a large handful of teabags. He stopped and turned slowly back towards me as I walked over and placed the teabags in his thin hand. For a long moment he stared at them with expressionless eyes, then turned his hand over and let them fall to the ground. He turned to go again.

"What's the matter?" I asked him, "Don't you want tea?"

He stared at me with a look of total bewilderment, but still said nothing. I had spoken in the local language, but began to wonder if he had perhaps not understood what I had said.

"Open them," Mohamed called from behind me. "He has probably never seen a teabag before."

I picked up the fallen white squares, tore one open, and poured the contents into the palm of my hand. Mohamed brought an empty tin can and I tipped the tea into it. As more bags were torn open and decanted, comprehension dawned and the old man's eyes lit up. He watched closely as all the fallen bags were retrieved and their contents added to the tin. When I held the tin out to him, he took it hesitantly and peered inside. Then, with a wrinkled black finger, he slowly stirred the dry leaves. He looked up and the eyes that met mine twinkled with delight.

Yusuf brought another tin with some sugar in it and gave it to the man, receiving a nod of thanks, but, again, no words. Mohamed brought one of our goatskin water bags and refilled the old man's battered kettle. When the lid had been replaced, our mysterious visitor looked at each of us in turn, nodded once and then, without any further acknowledgement, turned and walked away again, soon vanishing into the scrub.

We stood for a long time, staring after him in silence.

Our reverie was broken by another series of harsh barks from the baboons across the river. I looked quizzically at Mohamed. He knew the area and its people well. Surely there must be an explanation. The best part of an hour had passed since the old man had appeared and in that time he had spoken less than a dozen words.

A hundred questions filled my mind. Mohamed must have sensed my confusion.

"He is a man of passage," he said, as if this explained everything.

"A what?" Yusuf and I asked together.

"A man of passage," repeated Mohamed quietly, pausing for a moment before going on to explain: "His family are all dead. His animals have all been taken by raiders. He has no possessions, nothing more than what you see."

"Then how on earth does he survive?" I asked. "Where does he get food and shelter?"

"Oh, he will be fed and looked after wherever he goes by people who know of him, know his story and know that he has nothing." replied Mohamed. "He goes from place to place and never has to beg. People give him what they can without being asked. They recognise him for what he is – a man of passage."

The Visa

The livid purple date stamp on the covering letter showed that the invitation had arrived at the beginning of August. It had then lain in a filing tray on the big table in the middle of the office, hidden underneath a pile of other papers that had been put aside there because nobody knew quite what to do with them – or, more likely, didn't *want* to know what to do with them. It was now the last week in November.

I had come direct from the airport with the intention of handing in my report and then disappearing into the countryside for some well earned leave. There I stood, clutching a bunch of exotic tropical blooms for the girls in the office in one hand, and with a bulging suitcase full of dirty laundry in the other. My report was tucked under the strap that prevented the battered case from disgorging its contents all over the floor.

The boss was out when I arrived, but he had left a message for me. At least I was expected this time! That was something of a novelty.

"Gerald has been called up to see the Director," Caroline informed me. "Some Tanzanian fellow has turned up out of the blue and there's a bit of a stink about it. Gerald says he wants to see you as soon as he gets back and has suggested that you go through the limbo tray in the meantime to see if any of it concerns you." She paused, adding with a smile: "Thanks for the flowers. Can I get you some coffee?"

"Yes, please," I replied, fumbling in my pocket and handing her a coin for the machine down the corridor. "No sugar. Ta."

She click-clacked her way to the door as I sat down at the centre table to rummage through a two-foot-high pile of folders and loose papers. Most of them were from the Asian departments, who always seemed to have a bunch of loose schemes floating about. Much of the rest related to Latin America and looked a bit more interesting, but that was not my patch. They ought to be in separate trays, I thought.

Caroline came back with a clatter of high heels and placed the insipid brew beside me. "Bum!" she muttered. "That coin you gave – it was foreign."

"Sorry," I apologised, groping in my pocket again and finding an English one for her. I glanced down at the stiletto heels on which she was teetering. "You shouldn't wear those things," I remarked, teasingly. "They'll deform your feet."

"At least they won't give me frostbite," she shot back, looking pointedly at my sandals.

I stared down at them, moodily. Perhaps it was time I bought some proper shoes, I thought. And some socks.

"Where are you staying?" Caroline enquired. "Fancy coming back to my place for supper?" Her long fingers began to massage the back of my neck.

"Not this time, thanks. I'm off on leave as soon as I've seen Gerald and given him the word," I said over my shoulder as I picked up the crested envelope that lay at the very bottom of the pile.

"Going anywhere interesting?" she asked brightly as I slit open the envelope. "And can I come too?"

"I'm going to the West Country," I said vaguely, my attention now on the card. "And I'm going alone. You need to stay here where you belong so that you can concentrate on finding me an interesting project for the next trip."

"Pig!" she pouted. "You always say that. You never see any of the girls outside the office and you avoid all my advances, even when I more or less offer myself on a plate! Are you sure you're normal?"

"No. Spent too long living in mud huts," I grinned. "I'm trying to become a misogynist."

Caroline giggled and clicked her way back to her own desk. Annie now joined in the chit-chat from her desk on the other side of the room. "I reckon he's got one of those big black mammas out there in his mud hut. Twenty stone with boobs like socks full of sand! And flat feet from never wearing proper shoes! I'm told that's what happens to blokes when they spend as much time in places like that as he has."

Caroline chuckled. "Either that or some bead-jiggling, bone-tossing witch doctor has put a hex on him and eliminated all his normal desires," she suggested.

"Who said they were ever normal?" chortled Annie. "Not much of the rest of him is!"

This sort of good-natured banter continued for several minutes, with the other girls in the office joining in to offer their amusing, but friendly observations on the state of my morals, desires, preferences and habits. I listened with half an ear and enjoyed the warm feeling of acceptance that it gave me. However, my attention was now focused mainly on the invitation that I had withdrawn from the crested envelope.

The card, beautifully embossed on expensive pasteboard, invited us to send two delegates to an international conference to be held in Accra during the first week of December. The small print at the bottom requested an RSVP by 30th October, to the Minister of Foreign Affairs in Accra. Stapled to the card was a form to be returned to the High Commission in London. Scrawled across it, in brilliant turquoise ink, was an instruction to fill in the names of our delegates in the blank spaces on both the form and the invitation.

Gerald came back a few minutes later and called me into the rat hole he used as an office. I picked up my report, which I had typed on the Customs Inspector's antiquated machine in Monrovia while I waited for my overdue flight, and followed him in. He pushed a pile of papers off the spare chair onto an already overflowing side table and motioned me to take a seat. I dropped the report on his desk and lowered myself onto the chair.

Gerald flipped through the fifteen pages of closely typed details before carefully studying the conclusions and recommendations at the end.

"Not bad," he said eventually, closing the folder and reaching for his pipe. "You seem to have pulled everything together quite nicely." This, from Gerald, was as near as one was likely to get to thanks or praise. "Any unusual problems?" A cloud of acrid smoke billowed from his pipe as he puffed it into life.

"Not really. Only the usual muddle that keeps the Dark Continent afloat," I replied, turning the invitation card over in my hand.

"Good. Anything for you in the limbo tray?" The old swivel chair creaked loudly as he leaned back.

"No, but I did find this," I replied, offering him the card. "I'm afraid it's a bit late to do anything about it now."

He leaned forward and took the invitation. "Oh, I see what you mean – it's for next week," he said, looking concerned. "I wonder when it came in?" I decided not to mention how long it had been lying hidden in the in-tray. He thought for a moment and then added: "It is rather short notice, but we had better put in an appearance. It would look bad if we didn't show up."

Gerald did not like things to look bad. He leaned back in his protesting chair again and stared out of the grimy third floor window at the slanting rain that had been bathing the metropolis all afternoon. I was about to point out how long ago the invitation had been received, but he held up a hand to forestall my interruption.

"You'll have to go," he said with an air of finality. "Who do you want to take with you?"

"Oh, come on, Gerald," I protested. "You know I'm supposed to be going on four weeks' leave and you actually owe me four months altogether. It's just not on. I want time to visit my family, sink a few pints and do my laundry before I even think about going overseas again."

"Well, someone has to go," he said testily. "It's in your patch, and you're the only one who is free at the moment." He took another puff on his pipe and then, with a rather meaningful glance, added: "You could take Caroline if you like."

"Well, thanks, but I don't like!" I retorted.

Despite the fact that Caroline was great fun, and although she had a number of very obvious attractions and would undoubtedly be a useful assistant, her presence would not compensate for having to sit through a week of boring monologues about population problems and demographic demarcations when I should have been enjoying myself on holiday and taking the opportunity to catch up with my family. Nor could I raise any enthusiasm for the task of reading, understanding and summarising half a ton of irrelevant bumf so that some mindless bureaucrat in a London grotto could have a five-page synopsis with which to polish his pompous ego. I said as much to Gerald and watched him pull down the 'not listening' signs as he sat back and allowed me to get it out of my system.

I knew that Gerald would win in the end. He invariably did, but one had to try. "Why can't whatsisname go from Nairobi?" I pleaded, adding lamely: "This sort of thing is his special field." It was a rather feeble last stand and, anyway, Gerald had already made up his mind.

"He's rather busy just now – to do with that bod from Tanzania who was with the Director today." He took another puff on his pipe and then leaned forward and placed it in the ash tray, at the same time rising from his chair with an air of finality.

"That's settled then. You'll go out on your own. As it happens, we need you in Lama-Kara by the fifteenth, so it will all fit in very nicely. You can then have your couple of months, or whatever it is, when you come back in March." Gerald liked things to 'fit in nicely'. "Are you sure you don't want to take Caroline with you? She really ought to get out of the office and you are rather good at managing to look after less experienced bods in the field," he said, spoiling any attempt at magnanimity.

"I don't want to take anyone with me," I insisted angrily, still seething at the way I had had this extra duty foisted upon me. "I don't want to go at all. Anyway you can't seriously be suggesting that Caroline, who's never been further than Knightsbridge, should be asked to go with me to a place like Lama-Kara?" As I prepared to leave I added: "And, by the way, it will be five months you owe me by March."

"No, it won't," he looked startled. "You get paid, don't you? Look, get your visa tomorrow and I'll have Annie book your flight. You should fly out on Tuesday. That will give you the weekend free. Lama-Kara is being discussed at the Director's Committee on Monday afternoon. We'll need you there for the operational stuff. Three o'clock, eighth floor. Bring Caroline and her shorthand pad to keep the minutes."

"She's not a secretary," I protested.

"Quite right. That's why we should be able to get her into the meeting as one of our operatives. She may not be a secretary, but she's the only person in the department who can write shorthand at speed and still read the bloody stuff afterwards. And if stubborn buggers like you would agree to shepherd her in the field once in a while she'd be even more useful. Now, go and get that damned visa and sort out your laundry or whatever it was you wanted to get done. I'll see you on Monday at three." He waved me out of his lair with a gesture that brooked no further argument.

Closing the rat hole door behind me, I called out to Caroline: "What's for supper, then?"

"What? Wow! Did you hear that Annie? The iceman is melting! Gerald must really have given him a roasting." She danced a quick jig around her desk and then sat down again with a satisfied smirk.

"You ought to come back with me. I'm much better in bed," Annie said with a grin that told too much.

"Who said anything about bed, Annie? I'm only going for supper. But right now I'm going up to Accounts."

I turned back to Caroline: "Could you be an angel and ring the Okefield Hotel? Fix me a room for tonight and also for Monday night." And with that, I headed for the door, leaving the two girls to exchange significant looks.

The following morning Caroline dropped me at the traffic lights and I walked up the road towards the Consulate of the Ghanaian High Commission. Pausing outside, I looked at my watch. Twenty past nine. The notice by the door announced that the office opened at nine. I tried the door. It was locked. Stepping back, I looked up at the flag to make sure that it was not being flown at half-mast before I rang the doorbell. I had been caught by that situation once before and it had been most embarrassing.

A bell jangled distantly in the bowels of the building and I released the brass button. After a few moments I heard muffled footsteps behind the heavy door, followed by the sound of bolts being drawn back. A key scraped in the lock and the door opened to reveal a dazzlingly pretty girl with skin like the finest milk chocolate, tightly plaited hair and enormous gold earrings.

"Yairs?" she asked, looking first at me, then up and down the street as if trying to avoid being seen by the milkman.

"I've come to get a visa," I announced.

"We not open. Come back ten o'clock," she answered with a glorious smile that could boil a cold gin and tonic.

"But the notice says that the visa office opens at nine."

"Iss tellin lies," countered the girl. "Consulate don't open till ten."

"But it says…" I began, only to be cut off short.

"Look. Out there it is England, and the damn notice tellin damn English lies. In here it is Ghana, an we know what is so. Visa office him open at nine. Consulate open at ten," she finished with another smile.

"But the visa office is inside the Consulate." Frustration rose a notch.

"Thaa's right." She seemed pleased that I had grasped this essential fact at last. "Now, come back at ten o'clock for you visa," she instructed me with another quick smile. The door closed and the bolts shot home. The key grated in the lock again as if to emphasise her point.

There was nothing more I could do, so I wandered down the street towards the gardens at the far end. The air was thin and chilled in the watery winter sunshine. A small flock of pigeons took wing as I passed through the wrought iron arch of the gate into the small park. Patches of frost still lay white on the grass where the sun had not yet touched the lawns. An old man, bedecked in rags, his hand clutching a carrier bag, was tossing scraps of bread to a fluttering flock of birds.

I wandered slowly along the gravel path, kicking at fallen leaves, thinking about the previous evening with Caroline and wondering if I should maybe have accepted Gerald's suggestion after all. We had had fun, despite my tiredness. She was pretty, vivacious, warm, and every inch the city girl. And yet probably I had been right; she would have been bored to tears at the conference and it would really not be practical to have her along at

Lama-Kara with everything else I was expected to do.

It would be rough enough up there for even the most experienced bush hands, and I somehow could not visualise Caroline squatting behind the nearest convenient bush for relief, sitting on her haunches to eat local food or sleeping on a grass mat on the floor of a crowded mud hut. It wasn't as if there was anything useful she could do there. Oh well… , I kicked savagely at a pile of dead leaves to vent my frustration, getting an aggrieved look from the gardener who was busily sweeping them up.

Sheepishly, I looked away from his silent rebuke, then glanced at my watch and headed back towards the gate. It was ten past ten when I reached the Consulate again. This time the door stood open. I went in.

"Yairs?" enquired the girl I had met earlier, from behind a half open panel on the left.

"I would like to get a visa."

"For Ghana?"

"Yes please."

"Down the passage, turn lef, sekan door. Plenty peepol waitin," she directed me in a sing-song voice, treating me to another of her delightful smiles.

I followed her instructions, knocked on the door, and went in.

The man sitting behind the desk was short, chubby, and something of a dandy. His skin was very black, in sharp contrast to the two rows of polished ivory that he displayed.

"Can I help you?" he enquired, brushing the lapel of his gaudy check sports jacket with a gold encrusted hand.

"Good morning. I would like to get a visa, please," I said.

"For Ghana?"

"Yes, please."

He reached into a large wooden box on the floor beside his desk and rummaged about in a jumbled mass of paper. Selecting a crumpled form, he handed it to me.

"Heeah iss a form. Go an fill it," he instructed. The gold encrusted hand indicated an adjoining room furnished with a G-Plan dining table and chairs.

I sat down to fill in the form. Name, address, age; Mother's name, address, age; Mother's maiden name, address, age; Father's name, address, age; Grandfather's name, address, status (If deceased reason of death), age. The same for Grandmother and any brothers, sisters or other 'directly close relatives inclusive all of childs of self'. They must be setting up in competition to Salt Lake City and going to compile my family tree, I thought.

There followed the usual details of passport, reason for the intended visit, duration of proposed sojourn in Ghana, sponsor, and so on.

I checked the form and then returned to the other room. Hard wooden chairs were ranged along three walls. Half of them were now occupied by smiling Africans, all well wrapped in scarves and heavy overcoats despite the over-efficient heating that kept the place at a steady eighty degrees.

The official behind the desk was busy talking to someone on the telephone, so I sat down on a vacant chair and watched him. He had the phone tucked between chin and shoulder and was twisting a pink plastic ruler in his chubby hands, a wide smile on his face as his gaze slowly swept the audience lining the walls. He chatted to his caller in a manner that suggested the conversation was principally composed of trivialities.

The call eventually ended and he replaced the receiver. Still twisting the pink plastic ruler between his chipolata fingers, the man beamed at me. It was a real Cheshire Cat grin and seemed to be fixed in place. After perhaps two minutes, he leaned forward and pointed at me with the ruler.

"What do you want?" he asked.

"I would like a visa, please," I said, rising and offering him the form I had just filled in.

He ignored the offer and bent to rummage in the wooden box again. Selecting another form he held it aloft in triumph for the audience to see, before proffering it to me.

"Heeah iss a form. Go an fill it." He gestured again towards the room where I had filled in the other form.

I looked at the form he was offering me. It was the same as the one I had just filled in. "But I have just filled in one of these," I said, offering the completed form again. He took it this time and placed the blank one in my hand. "Will you need any more?" I asked. "Perhaps you could give them to me now so that I can do them all at once."

"You muss fill dem separetly," he said, picking up the pink ruler again and pointing towards the next room.

I filled in the forms as they were rationed to me. Four in all, handed over and exchanged for a blank one as they were completed. Returning the final one, I gave him my passport as well, along with a pile of photographs with my name printed on the back of each one. The official placed the forms to one side and put the photographs in a neat pile in the centre of his polished desk. His smile expanded to watermelon proportions as he produced a huge pair of scissors with bright green handles from the desk drawer. With great care he proceeded to trim the little white borders of each of the photographs, depositing the clippings, piece by piece, in the waste basket.

I stood and watched, fascinated by the care he was taking and the totality of his concentration. When he had finished, and the photographs were once again in a neat pile, he returned the shears to their drawer and brought out a large pot of glue. With this he stuck one photograph onto each of the completed forms and then spread these in a line across the vast expanse of his desk.

He then opened my passport and studied the photograph. He looked from the passport to me several times to check that it was really mine, then compared the photographs on each of the forms with the passport, with me, and with each other.

Apparently satisfied that the pictures were indeed of me and that they were all the same, he took a heavyweight stapler from the desk drawer and thumped a staple into each one. Right across my nose. Ouch! Not satisfied with this effort at disfigurement, he selected a rubber stamp from the carousel and, pressing this firmly into an oozing red ink pad and breathing heavily on the inked surface, he stamped 'VERIFIED' across the middle of each of the four pictures. They were now all but invisible, but my fascination grew as he added his signature to each one with a coarse felt-tipped pen.

Now beaming even more broadly than ever, he sat back and

inspected his handiwork with satisfaction. He looked at me as if seeking my approval and I returned his grin with a thin smile as he picked up the gaudy pink plastic ruler again.

Next, he turned his attention to the forms. Clearing the surface of extraneous objects, he realigned them side by side across the middle of the desk. Meticulously, he checked the details entered on each form, ensuring that all four had been completely filled in and that they were all identical. Then he opened my passport and checked all four forms against that.

I pulled a chair over from the wall and sat down opposite him to watch. He continued, oblivious to my attention, tapping each section of each form with the pink plastic ruler as it was checked line by line. When he was finally satisfied that all was in order, he looked up and treated me to another spectacular display of ivory.

"What iss youah name?"

I told him. He looked down at the forms and placed a finger over my surname. With the pink ruler he pointed to my forenames and asked: "Who are dose people? You can only hab one man on one form and you hab puttin four."

"Those are my first names," I explained. He held my gaze for a few moments, as if digesting this information, before resuming his study of the forms. He stared fixedly at them for some time, preparing his next shot. It was beautiful.

"You can only hab one fers name." The smile was gone now. "So who are dees two persons?"

I pinched my leg, unwilling to believe that this was really happening. "Those are part of my name," I explained. "It is written there in my passport."

He picked up the small blue book and looked, comparing the passport again with each of the forms.

"Iss diss youah passport?" He tapped the little book with his ruler.

I've met a few, but this one was a five star lulu.

"Yes. This is my passport. That is my picture. And there is my name. You have just verified it on all those forms." I reached over and pointed to the blood red marks, hoping that he would not take it into his head to obliterate the picture in my passport in a similar manner.

He studied the forms again and compared each one carefully with the passport. The ruler twisted in his hands as he stared at the documents. When he looked up, his smile had been restored in all its glory.

"Daa's right!" he announced, and I felt a small flutter of relief. "So, diss iss youah name. An diss iss youah passport. So! Tell me, why do you want to go to Ghana?"

It was written on the forms, but I produced the invitation card and showed it to him.

"I am invited to attend this conference in Accra."

He took the card and read it carefully, then compared the name with the forms, and finally with the passport.

"Yairs. But why do you want to go to Ghana?"

He was at it again! This really could not be happening. It must be a dream, and a pretty lousy one at that. That's it, I was asleep and having a nightmare. I pinched my leg again to make sure. It hurt. It was real. I groaned inwardly as he went on.

"I muss know dees tings befoah I can be gib you any visa."

Slowly, I explained everything again from the beginning, with lots of gesticulation and prodding at the various documents arrayed between us to make sure that he understood and accepted each point. I finally petered out, hoping that he had got it this time.

"Ohhh Kay!" he said, with great expression, when I had finished. Once more he picked up the pink plastic ruler and used it as a pointer. "So, diss iss youah passport."

He prodded the book.

I nodded.

"An diss iss youah pikcha."

He prodded.

I nodded.

"An diss," he brandished the ruler with a flourish, "iss youah name."

I nodded again. "Yes." It came out as a croak.

With his free hand he picked up the embossed invitation card. "So!" He was enjoying this. "Wid diss passport," he tapped it with the ruler, "an diss one pikcha," he tapped again, "an diss name," tap again, "you want to go to Ghana for be go diss one conference, an you do be ask by diss one card." The card was waved in the air and he looked round to make sure that his audience had missed nothing and that they all understood my request.

"Yes." It was more a half-stifled sob than a word. I wished he would just give me the blasted visa and let me escape before I turned into a gibbering wreck.

He was not finished yet.

"Ohhh Kay!" There was a wicked glint in his eyes. "So! Tell me. Who do go ask you for go for diss ting?"

"It is an official invitation from your Minister of Foreign Affairs in Accra. It is printed on that card."

"So!" He held the card up for everyone in the room to see. "I see."

I fervently hoped that he did.

"You do go be guest of Govament, an diss one card he say it?" He prodded the card again with the pink plastic ruler.

"Yes." He really had understood at last. "Please, may I have a visa?"

He looked down at the card for a moment, then picked up all the papers, shuffled them together and tucked them inside the passport. He tossed the whole lot into a tray on the table behind him and picked up the pink ruler again. As he twisted it in his hands the ivory shone brightly and he delivered his verdict.

"You can come an take it in one week."

"But that will be too late. I have to be in Accra before that for the conference."

He thought about this for a moment. "So! You can come tomorrow," he offered helpfully.

"Tomorrow is Saturday. Your office is closed on Saturdays," I said.

"Monday," he adjusted the offer.

"Please, can I have it today?" I pleaded.

He twisted the pink plastic ruler and looked around at his audience. "You can come at tree o'clock," he relented, "an we shall see."

"Thank you. Thank you." I shook his hand vigorously and left in search of a restorative.

When I returned at three o'clock the front door was open, so I walked in and headed down the passage.

"Yairs?" called the girl with the earrings, as I passed her hatch.

"I've come for my visa. I know the way, thanks," I said, keeping going.

"Down the passage, turn lef, sekan door. Plenty peepol waitin." Her chant floated after me as I turned the corner, knocked and opened the door.

The official was still at his desk, still smiling and still turning the pink plastic ruler in his fat little hands. That ruler is going to feature in all my worst nightmares from now on, I thought, closing the door behind me to keep the heat in. The same audience that had witnessed the earlier proceedings was still seated round the walls, still wrapped for the arctic.

"Can I help you?" asked the official. Just as he had in the morning, he dusted his spotless lapels with his gold encrusted fingers.

"I've come to collect my visa," I told him.

"For Ghana?"

Something was all too horribly familiar. "That's right. I came in this morning and you asked me to come back at three."

"Ohhh yairs." More ivory.

I waited.

After a few moments he reached forward and lifted my papers from a tray on the front of his desk. This was progress, I thought. At least they had progressed from in the tray behind him. He spread out the forms and opened my passport.

"What iss youah name?" he asked, looking up at me.

I flinched.

"An why do you want to go to Ghana?"

We went through the whole thing again. Twice.

Finally the man pushed back his chair, stood up, and left the room, telling me to wait.

I pulled the hard wooden chair from its place by the wall and sat down opposite the desk, thinking that the next time Gerald could go to the damned conference himself and get his own blasted visas. I waited. The muffled figures around the room were chatting in animated undertones. Occasionally, one of them would look in my direction and flash that same Cheshire Cat grin. All the others would then stop chatting and grin at me. It was a disease!

Twenty minutes later the official returned carrying a polished wooden box, which he placed reverently on the desk before taking his seat. More ivory as he picked up the pink plastic ruler.

"Iss diss youah passport?" He pointed with the ruler.

"Yes."

"An you are ask for visa?" He prodded the passport again.

"Yes, please."

"For Ghana?"

Not again, please! "Yes," I somehow managed to sound calm.

He opened the passport and selected a double blank page near the middle, folding the little book back on itself until the spine cracked and it lay flat on the desk. Taking another sodden ink pad from the drawer – black this time, I noticed – he opened the polished box. From this he took out a large and very official looking stamp with which he vigorously assaulted the squelching pad. This activity attracted the attention of those seated round the room. His intense concentration hushed them as he placed the stamp carefully over the blank page. His grin expanded as he raised his hand above his head and slammed it down on the stamp with enough force to make the wooden box jump on the desk. Slowly he lifted the stamp off the passport and replaced it in the box before inspecting his handiwork.

I was surprised, given the state of the ink pad, to see that the impression was remarkably clear. It evidently met with the official's approval for he produced a revenue stamp and affixed it to the corner of the page, scrawled his signature across it and wrote something in a space on the new impression.

Once again he inspected his handiwork, then snapped the passport closed. Picking up the invitation card, he handed them both to me with another show of teeth.

"I hab to make it check, you know. Iss juss to make it shuah dat iss all orite."

I nodded and took the passport. "Thank you," I mumbled, hardly daring to believe that the ordeal was over. I stood up and shook the official's hand. Muttering my thanks again, I headed for the door.

As I reached out for the doorknob he fired his parting salvo.

"You do go be guest of Govament?"

"Yes."

"Ifin you do go be guest of Govament you no do go need no visa."

Sankarani

Coming out of Senegal on my way to Bougouni in southern Mali, I encountered heavy rain and floods that had left the normal route almost completely washed out. My only option was to turn south, crossing into Mali at Satadougou. The minor roads through the northern fringes of the Tinkisso country were in better condition, partly because they were over high ground, but also because they carried fewer heavy vehicles.

At Sitakoto, the locals told me that the roads were again washed out. I had come by this southern route to avoid a seven-hundred-kilometre detour northwards through the edge of the Sahara. Now it looked as if I might have to make another long loop through the capital, Bamako, in order to get to Bougouni. I decided, instead, to turn south again and see if it was possible to sneak through the north-east corner of Guinea. The border was only a few kilometres down the road from where I was and I would not be in the country for long.

The border guards were friendly enough, but since I had no visa for their country they said that one of them would have to accompany me to Siguiri to get my papers authorised there. After that, there should be no problem about my passing briefly through Guinea and back into Mali. However, I realised that there were no guarantees. There was always the risk that I might be turned back at the other end, in which case I would have wasted even more days. Apart from that, it was also quite possible that the suggestion of first going to Siguiri to get my papers signed was simply an excuse for one of the guards to get a ride into town.

I asked if there might not be some other way, but the man in charge insisted that I should go to Siguiri. The discussion went back and forth for half an hour, lubricated with numerous cups of bitter black tea until, eventually, one of the guards slung his rifle over his shoulder and picked up a large, closely woven basket, indicating that the debate was now ended and we should get going.

Outside, I opened the canvas cover of the pick-up and the guard tossed his basket in. It landed roughly, emitting loud squawks that betrayed the presence of the chickens within. I looked quizzically at the soldier, who smiled and shrugged.

"The others will eat them while I am gone, so if I wish to keep them I must take them with me," he explained as I pulled down the canvas flap and lashed it firmly in place.

Corporal Siméon Djinga turned out to be unusually well educated given the limited extent of schooling generally available in the area. He was extremely knowledgeable about the region, even though he was not a local, and asked a lot of interesting questions about the neighbouring countries I had visited. The conversation was relaxed and made a pleasant change from my normal solo travels.

I had forgotten to set the milometer when we set off, but the total distance of the trip must have been about one hundred-and-eighty kilometres. The road was little used and had not been well maintained over recent years. Long stretches were heavily overgrown and the season's rains had caused deep erosion in some parts. As a result, the journey took us nearly seven hours, much of it in low ratio second gear. The four wheel drive had certainly earned its keep on this occasion.

When we reached Siguiri, Siméon asked me to stop at a bar. The crafty charmer then conned me into paying for the beer. This wasn't too difficult as I, too, was parched. Despite the fact that it was nearly four o'clock in the morning, the beer still tasted like nectar. However, fifteen hundred francs did seem rather excessive for two cold beers, even at that unsociable hour – and even allowing for the fact that this was a small provincial town, where everything inevitably cost a bit more than in the cities.

After we'd downed the first beer, Siméon found someone to cook for us and we were soon tucking into steaming bowls of bean soup, pieces of some stringy fowl in a hot sauce, and sour milk. Nobody asked me to pay for this, or for subsequent beers, and I realised that the fifteen hundred francs had been an all-inclusive deal. No doubt some share of the profit would end up in

Siméon's pocket, but, by the time we had finished the meal, I felt it had been excellent value.

The woman who had been serving us was tall and thin, with attentive eyes and a ready smile. She brought us small glasses of thick syrupy coffee and dry bread as dawn started to brighten the eastern horizon.

Administrative offices in this part of Africa do not open until nine at the earliest and often much later, so we dozed in low-slung string chairs, sleeping off our feast. By nine, the day was hot and steamy and I was keen to get the formalities done as soon as possible. Siméon appeared to be in no hurry. He told me that the official we needed to see never came to his office before noon, and that, anyway, he wanted to visit the market first.

I began to feel a bit as if I were being used. It also crossed my mind that he might be banking on my entry being refused, since this would mean I would have to go back the way I had come, enabling him to get a lift back to the border post as well, having done whatever it was he had to do in town. However, it was too late for recriminations, so I told him to go off to the market. I, meanwhile, would go to find some fuel and would meet him back at the bar at noon. We would then go to the Prefecture and get my papers stamped.

Siméon was delighted. His eyes twinkled, his face twisted into a broad, conspiratorial grin, and he shambled off down an alley and disappeared. It was only when I climbed into the driving seat that I found Siméon had left his rifle in the cab. It could be difficult for both of us if I were to be found with that, so I climbed down and gave it to the woman in the bar. She took it as though this were a normal occurrence and I was left wondering if there was more than a casual acquaintance between her and Siméon.

The only source of fuel in Siguiri turned out to be on the other side of the river, and the only bridge had been washed away the previous year. This was the mighty Niger River. Mighty? Well, it may have been lower downstream at Mopti, Timbuktu, or down at the delta in far away Nigeria. Here, however, it was less impressive, no more than a shallow muddy flow, about a hundred metres wide, that was nevertheless running fast and full from the heavy rains that should have ended some weeks before.

A helpful boy soon told me that the only way across was by ferry. It turned out that there was a timber mill about a kilometre downstream with a good ferry that served both the mill and the public. It was inevitable that the ferry had just reached the far bank when I arrived, and it was more than an hour before I finally managed to get across.

The filling station, when I found it, turned out to belong to the timber company. To call it a filling station was a rather flattering description. It consisted of a tin shack, made from flattened oil drums that had been wired together, in which were stored a collection of dented 40-gallon drums of petrol and diesel. There was a hand pump, but this was broken, so the fuel had to be dispensed by means of standing one drum on top of another and then siphoning the contents from that into a five-litre can and thence into the fuel tank. Basic, but it worked.

My last jerrycan had just been filled when the engineer from the mill arrived, having heard that a white man had turned up. Although he, too, was white, his origin was obscure and he spoke with an accent that I could not recognise. His name also remained a mystery; he was apparently known to everyone simply as 'Chef'.

He was curious about my journey and asked about the condition of the roads I had used. He was most amused when he heard that I was hoping to get my papers signed at the Prefecture and told me that even for such a short transit as I was proposing, this could only be done at Kankan, some two hundred kilometres in the opposite direction to that in which I was heading. Now that I had crossed the river, the idea of just carrying on suddenly became rather attractive. I asked what he thought.

"There will be no problem," he said. "The Corporal will be disappointed not to have a ride back to his post, and someone will probably come over here to look for you, but they won't go any further." His experience over many years in this isolated place had made him disdainful of administrative niceties. He added, deadpan: "The ferry will break down this afternoon and I will not mend it for two days. Then they will not bother." The mischief that twinkled in his eyes as he spoke was echoed in his tone of voice. Here was a friend.

The engineer invited me to eat with him and then offered to provide me with a guide who would show me the best route as far as Sankarani. He had a man working for him who came from that area, who had not been home for a long time and who would be only too pleased to go with me.

I looked on the map, but could not find Sankarani marked. It could be either a vast empty tract or just two huts in the middle of nowhere. I was a bit doubtful. The idea of having a good guide was certainly very attractive, but I needed to have some idea about where exactly our destination lay.

"It is not far from Badougou and Yanfolia," replied Chef, when I inquired. "It's about one hundred miles inside Mali. You will know it when you are there."

I looked on the map again but could find neither of the two other places he had mentioned. Moreover, there were no roads, nor even any tracks marked heading east from Siguiri. Chef assured me that I would be heading in the direction I wished to go and that the country was easily navigable. The man he proposed as my guide knew it well and was very reliable. After we reached Sankarani, it would be only a couple of hours' drive further east to the Bougouni road, and I could hardly miss that. He made it sound very easy and straightforward.

What the hell, I thought? I'll take a chance and go for it. I felt a twinge of guilt about Siméon and hoped he wouldn't get into too much trouble for letting me escape. However, this thought vanished as fast as it had formed, for it was probable that Siméon had not told anyone in authority that I was there in the first place. I dismissed him from my mind and accepted the offer of a guide. Chef was delighted and went to find his man.

The driving became easier after the first half hour. Gently rolling savannah, dotted with spindly, flat-topped acacia and occasional knobbly karite trees, stretched as far as the eye could see. There were gullies where run-off from the rains had engraved the red earth during the wet season, but these were mostly shallow and easily crossed. Periodically, we passed rocky outcrops or clusters of oddly-shaped anthills, like rusting fairy castles. There was no sign of people anywhere, but occasional flashes of brilliant colour among the bushes signalled the presence of exotically decorated birds that had been disturbed by our passage.

My guide was a wizened little man with closely cropped hair and a torn right ear. We shared no common language and he made do with occasional grunts and gestures to indicate the direction I should follow. Most of the time, he maintained an air of studied boredom as he watched the passing countryside.

The sun was setting behind us, casting a long shadow in front of the truck. My guide suddenly sat up straight in his seat and pointed to a gap between two thorn bushes. He began to chatter excitedly as I turned in the direction he had indicated.

"Sankarani! Sankarani!" he shouted as we burst out of the thicket.

I had to stamp hard on the brakes, throwing us both forward as the vehicle came to a halt, nose down on a crumbling bank that sloped down to a full brown watercourse a few metres in front of us. Muddy water a hundred metres wide stretched out into the distance on either side of us, flowing gently northwards.

If it was marked on any map at all, it appeared as nothing more than a dry gully, but there was no denying the existence of this large river. My guide was now in a state of high excitement. He grabbed my arm from the steering wheel whilst bouncing up and down on his seat like an excited four-year old. With his free hand he was pointing towards the water just in front of our wheels, yelling: "Sankarani! Sankarani!" His face was split by a toothless grin, his eyes bright with delight as though he were Stanley meeting Livingstone. He really was a delightful fellow and his excitement was infectious. I began to laugh with him.

All of a sudden, he then released my arm and started to behave as if he was suffering an attack of fleas, scrabbiting about inside the front of his clothing like a demented monkey. This spasm ceased as suddenly as it had begun and his hand emerged clutching a small bundle wrapped in glossy *shinga'a* leaves. He unwrapped them to reveal two fat pink *kola* nuts.

With another toothless grin, he gave me one of the nuts. To my slight alarm, his hand was then thrust once again into the front of his clothing. After several moments of energetic searching, he withdrew a second leaf-wrapped bundle, neatly bound with a strip of bark. He untied the package to display a set of gleaming stainless steel false teeth. These were promptly pushed into his mouth and he bit into the second *kola* nut.

My astonishment evidently delighted him and his face performed an intricate choreography of smiles and grimaces. His humorous eyes glowed like hot coals in the last of the sunlight that was being reflected off the water in front of us.

I bit into my kola nut and we chewed together in companionable silence for the few brief minutes of the African dusk. My friend – I could definitely call him that now that we had shared his kola nuts – periodically muttered "Sankarani" between bites. His tone was hushed, almost mystical, as if this place held some sacred significance for him.

We sat there chewing contentedly as the light faded. The birdsong, which had been so loud before sunset, diminished to a twitter and finally to silence. It was replaced a few minutes later by the strident nocturnal insect chorale. Overhead, the sky dimmed rapidly from gold to crimson-streaked indigo and finally to black. Through the clear, still air the stars shimmered brightly, as if millions of fireflies were courting in the endless void.

After our long afternoon's drive, I felt completely at peace as we sat nibbling our kola nuts under the dark vault. Presently, my companion climbed down from the cab and vanished into the darkness without a word. I wondered idly whether I should follow, or had he left me? I felt a flutter of uncertainty flow through me. Would he just disappear, like a shadow when the sun goes behind a cloud, now that we had reached Sankarani and his duty was done?

As silently as he had slipped away, my friend materialised at my elbow some minutes later. His arms were laden with firewood. On top of the pile lay two wild melons and a large fruit rat, minus its head. I had no idea how he had been able to obtain these items for he had no weapon, we were more than a hundred and eighty kilometres from anywhere and we had not seen a soul since leaving the timber mill at Siguiri. By whatever means he had managed it, his foraging had been carried out without the slightest sound.

Restarting the engine, I reversed the vehicle back through the thorn bushes onto a clear patch of level ground. My friend dumped his load on the ground and searched around the clearing where it was illuminated by the headlights. Within a few minutes, he had located three suitable stones that he brought together to form a hearth. Laying a fire in this took only a few moments and I was about to reach into the vehicle for some matches when he produced a shiny Zippo lighter from the folds of his garment and ignited the twigs. His clothing seemed to contain an Aladdin's cave of useful items and I wondered what else he had secreted in there.

Before I could see how he had done it, the skin was removed from the huge rodent – without the use of a knife. He took the one that I offered and cut the meat into small chunks. Selecting sticks from the pile that he had collected, he then fashioned a set of skewers. He had stoked the fire with some more substantial fuel and as the flames died down to glowing embers he laid the skewered meat on top, covering it with thick, glossy leaves torn from the bush beside him. Moments later, there were clouds of dense smoke and the pungent smell of sizzling meat and aromatic leaves. While he was hunched over the cooking, I found my kettle and filled it with water from one of the vehicle's tanks. I added a handful of tea and some sugar. I also had some corncobs, which we tossed onto the embers, still wrapped in their husks. This was going to be a good feast, complete with fresh meat, corn, fruit, and hot tea.

After we had eaten our fill and were sitting beside the fire sipping sweet tea, I tried to ask the man how he had caught the rodent. He looked puzzled at first, but finally, by performing a ridiculous dance and mime, which obviously delighted and amused him, I made him understand and he nodded vigorously as comprehension dawned.

Once again, his hand delved deep into his clothing and he brought out a short tubular leather case. From the case he took a piece of sorghum stalk about a foot long and another leaf wrapped bundle. This contained a dozen small darts made from grass stems, with large thorns stuck in one end. Several small pieces of ostrich plume were bound on just behind the thorn to serve as flights, with a knot of raw cotton twisted onto the other end. He mimed putting the dart into the sorghum stalk and then held this to his mouth. A blowpipe! An unusual weapon for Africa, but this was an unusual man.

Having put his huntsman's tools away, he then disappeared once more into the bushes. This time he made no attempt to keep quiet and I could hear him moving about in the darkness some way off. After a while, he returned with a long dry sorghum stalk, squatted by the fire, and added more wood to the embers, blowing them swiftly into a dancing blaze.

Using my knife, he cut an intricate criss-cross pattern down the length of the hollow sorghum stalk. Towards one end he bored a line of large holes on one side. Humming quietly to himself, he inspected his work critically in the firelight. Satisfied, he held the carved stalk in the flames, rotating it and moving it backwards and forwards until it appeared to be darkly scorched along its entire length. In a few minutes it was done and he began to scrape away the char, leaving the stalk bright and clean except for the dark lines of the pattern he had cut into it.

Measuring three spans of his hand from the opposite end of the stalk to that with the holes, he cut that section off, held it to his mouth and blew sharply, just as he had with his blowpipe. Looking at me for the first time since he had started work, he grinned. It was simplicity itself.

Laying aside the new blowpipe, he picked up the longer piece of stalk with the holes cut in it, held it against his nostril and exhaled steadily. The improvised flute emitted a low reedy note. Taking up the knife again, he made some adjustments and trimmed a little off the end of the stalk. Once he was satisfied, he proceeded to play a long haunting tune that held me spellbound in the flickering firelight.

As the fire dwindled, my unnamed friend indicated that he would sleep now. I pulled a couple of blankets from a locker in the back of the pick-up and offered him one, indicating that he could sleep on top of the canvas tilt. He climbed up, rolled himself in the blanket and was instantly asleep.

I climbed up beside him and lay on the canvas where it formed a flat hammock between the frames. Sleep would not come and I lay on my back staring up at the star-spangled sky, my mind filled with a stream of vivid images that formed a jumbled kaleidoscope of the day's events.

Sleep must have taken me eventually for I woke in the chill before dawn with something digging into my back. There was nobody beside me, with the result that the canvas had sagged and I was now resting on the spare fuel cans below. The other blanket was there, neatly rolled and bound with a broad strip of *wiwe* bark, tied in a decorative knot. Tucked under the bark strap was a small package of *shinga'a* leaves. I unwrapped it and found another *kola* nut.

Realising that he really had gone for good this time, I climbed down and rekindled the fire to make tea. Beside the hearth lay the flute and the blowpipe that the man with the steel teeth had fashioned the night before. Next to these, in a neat row, lay my knife and one delicate grass-stemmed dart.

The light increased as I made the tea and thought about how I should proceed from here. I toasted another corncob for breakfast and thought about the previous day's events. For the first time since leaving the timber mill, I wondered what had happened to Siméon and hoped he had not got into trouble. I thought about my extraordinary guide and marvelled at his friendship and generosity.

As the sun rose I saw there was a stick thrust into the ground in front of the vehicle. The top had been split and bent over with part of the end turned back like curled fingers. One twig stuck out like a grotesque finger, pointing north along the riverbank.

Sphinx

The sombre masses of brooding black cloud were gone. In their place, the bright stars twinkled, silent and timeless. The fury of the electrical storm, with its heaving, swirling ocean of clouds constantly rent by savage slashes of lightning, had felt as though it would never end. But the sonorous rumbling thunder, which yields no rain to the parched landscape, had grumbled its last.

Now, in the pre-dawn calm, the thick, tortured air that had seemed to suffocate existence itself had cooled and stilled so that a shallow sea of ground mist lay like a limp blanket about the ankles of the sparse desert scrub. Grotesque spindly shapes rose above the still whiteness and were dimly visible in the faint luminescence cast by the myriad silver pinpricks in the black heavens.

The young man sat motionless, staring out over the silent countryside. The moon, now only a memory, had set some hours before, driven to its rest by the fury of the storm. In this calm monochrome world, even the stars were starting to fade. As they were extinguished one by one, he waited for the dim grey seam of light that would gradually appear, dividing the fickle heavens from the endless arid earth. It would herald the coming dawn and presage another day of scorching sun combined with the interminable, searing wind that blows from the distant lava fields, dessicating everything in its path. Thirst would soon follow, the fine wind-borne dust caking the moist tissues of mouth and nose.

Some distance to his right, the silence was shattered by the harsh bark of a prowling jackal. An answering call came a few moments later, from further away. The hyena will be the next to make itself heard, he mused, and as if in response to his thought, the strange hooted howl of the mangy scavenger echoed faintly in the still air, but remained unanswered.

The young man shivered, waiting impatiently for the daylight that would enable him to continue his search for the beguiling, long-legged beauty who had come to obsess him and whose disappearance had brought him to this spot.

It had been almost six weeks since he had last seen her wandering forlorn and alone in the gathering dusk. At first, he had just watched. Then, fascinated, he had tried to follow. He had even called out to her, but his call had gone unheeded and she had stalked off without even looking round to acknowledge his presence. He felt sure that she had been aware of him, had heard his call, and yet she had ignored him. In the gathering gloom he had carelessly walked into a thorn bush and by the time he had disentangled himself she was gone and he had been unable to find her footprints in the darkness.

With a touch of sadness, he had retraced his steps, unable to get her out of his mind. He thought of the graceful way that she carried her head; the gentle, smooth curves of her neck, back and shoulders; the slim elegance of her legs. He felt her loneliness and shared it. He longed to console her, knowing that it was impossible.

Those feelings were with him still, but mixed now with a sense of foreboding as he sat and waited, wondering if this would be the day he would see her again and fearful as to whether she was still even alive. He ached with the longing to find her unharmed as he whiled away the few remaining minutes of tranquillity that would soon be shattered by the onslaught of the new day.

He shifted his position and winced in pain. He had remained virtually motionless for many hours throughout the long night and his joints had stiffened. Slowly he rose, stretching each cramped limb in turn before resuming his seat on the crumbling old anthill.

The jackal barked again. It was answered by a long drawn out squeal from its mate, closer this time. The stars were vanishing ever more rapidly and the thin grey line that marked the horizon was growing more distinct. The young man raised his right hand in front of him, palm forward, with his two outer fingers extended and just discernible against the dim horizon.

The time of the horns.

Dawn. Not long now and he could resume his search. He felt

the grip of hunger and remembered that he had eaten almost nothing for the last three days. He wondered if she had managed to survive out there on her own and, if so, how she was faring.

This one-sided love affair had begun seven months before. To distract his mind from a private tragedy at home, the young man had come to this desolate place to work. By pouring all his energies into helping a people decimated by drought and unable to help themselves, he had submerged his grief and allowed it, slowly, to heal. When he had first arrived, he had done nothing for a long time. He had wandered around, learning a few words of the local language, and gradually people had grown accustomed to his presence. He had made his camp near their encampment – but not too close – so that they could see and observe him from a comfortable distance.

At first, his tent had been the subject of much comment and discussion, with more than a little amusement one day when it had blown down. The people had helped him to put it up again and that had been the beginning of their friendship. Soon they were bringing him fresh milk each day. From then on, he had been made welcome as he wandered among the people and chatted.

Eventually, someone had asked him why he had come to live there without either goats or camels of his own. He had explained, but suspected that they understood little. They had looked mystified when he explained about the work he was there to do on their behalf and for which he was hoping to enlist their help, so he had made a model to show them what he had planned. The matter had been discussed for a long time, but an agreement had eventually been concluded and work had begun. Progress had been good, all things considered, and the people had proved to be willing workers, quick to learn.

The first thing the young man had done when he got there was to dig a well. As with much of what he did in those early days after his arrival, this had caused much comment and a great deal of amusement among the people. However, the regular clean water supply that resulted was soon appreciated, although it was insufficient for the number of people camped in the area. Before long, the young man had organised the digging of two more wells – one, close by, to provide more drinking water for the people and another, some distance away and complete with a trough, for their animals.

Everybody had lent a hand with these projects, the women and children as well as the men. They would work every morning until the midday heat made it uncomfortable and then, in the afternoons, the young man would treat any wounds or other ailments that he was capable of dealing with. During the evenings, he would join them around their flickering camp fires. The older folk would tell stories of past events and local lore, while the children would play and giggle, like children the world over, until they fell asleep. Sometimes the young man would tell them of his own country or of strange places he had visited in other lands, and slowly his command of the language grew to fluency.

In the end, the drought had won. Thanks to the new wells, there was plenty of water for the people and their animals, but the area had become over-grazed and the herds had to be driven further afield each day to find grass. Something would have to be done, so a meeting was called. Everyone came and even the children had the right to be heard. The discussion went on for two days and nights. Since the work had begun, food had been less of a problem than usual because the people were fed in return for their efforts. They were keen to carry on with the work, but their animals were still – and always would be – their principal source of livelihood and wealth and had to be provided for.

Eventually, a decision was arrived at. It was agreed that everyone would move north, further into the great depression, where there was still some good grazing. Later, some of them would return with the changing moon and resume the work. They departed three days after the new moon.

Left on his own, the young man's thoughts returned to the exotic beauty who had so captured his heart. He had first noticed her a few days after the people had originally agreed to start work on the project. He had been out with two of the men, scouting for a suitable site for a weir, when he saw her sitting alone in the shade of an isolated acacia tree. He had made some remark to his companions, but they had dismissed her, telling him not to worry about her. She was not their concern. They left each other alone, they said, and that way they could all live their lives in peace.

The philosophy of live and let live was strong among these people, except, that is, when the Issa came up from the south and raided their herds. Then bloody battles were fought, men died and women and children cried. Otherwise, their policy of peaceful co-existence extended to everyone around them, not just people but wildlife as well. Starving as they might be, they had no tradition of hunting, so the abundant game that shared their desert home was ignored as a potential source of food.

In the months that followed he had often seen her, sometimes alone, sometimes in the company of her husband – if, indeed, that's who he was. The pair would pass near to the work site, only to be completely ignored by everybody. Increasingly, the young man found that he couldn't get her out of his mind and he realised that he had started to develop a deep affection for her. She was slim and lithe and moved with feline grace. At some time in the past, her husband had suffered a broken ankle that had set quite well but had left him with an awkward gait that was distinctive, even at a distance.

After the people had moved away, the young man made up his mind to go in search of her. She had not been around for several weeks and this worried him. Also, he had noticed the last few times he had seen her that she had looked different in some subtle way that he was not quite able to identify. He hoped that she had not also moved on, along with the rest of the community. He visited all the places where he had seen her before, but there was no sign of her.

Nevertheless, something told him that she had not gone far away and might still be in the area. By now she had come to occupy his mind so frequently that he felt an almost obsessive need to find out more about her. He spent every spare moment searching for her. And then, three days after the last of the people had left, he found an ominous sign.

At first he thought it was a flake of obsidian glinting in the sun. Then, as he approached, he saw that it was a bright nickel cartridge case from a high powered rifle. He had heard distant shots the day before, but had not known their source. Now he felt his heart quicken with some vague fear. Thinking about it, he could define no good reason why he should have feared for her, but he had, momentarily.

He stood on the endless empty plain, casting no shadow under the midday sun as he tossed the tiny silver cylinder in his hand and looked all around. At first he saw nothing. Then a large rock some distance away caught his eye. Parts of the desert were littered with odd-shaped boulders that had been spat out by the volcano on the northern horizon in some past age. Just another rock, he thought, but as he turned away it appeared to move and he swung back to look more closely.

It was hard to see clearly through the shimmering heat haze, but the rock appeared to ripple in an unnatural way, as if disturbed by the breeze. His curiosity aroused, he started walking towards it to take a closer look. He was still some yards away when he suddenly realised that it was not a rock at all, but a dead ostrich, its plumes fluttering gently in the light breeze. And just beyond the ostrich lay another body that was all too familiar. At first, for one sickening moment, he thought it was her, but, moving closer, he saw that it was her husband.

He froze. Shivers of fear played 'hickory-dickory-dock' up and down his spine. Instinctively he crouched and spun round, shielding his eyes from the glare, scanning the empty horizon before moving closer.

Dark splashes of blood stained the ground around him and a dozen or more dark patches covered the skin where shot after shot had thumped into his body, snuffing out life and leaving no more than a lump of torn carrion for the vultures that would soon be circling overhead.

The young man bent to examine the body, gingerly touching the deformed ankle. A wave of panic passed through him and he looked around again, desperate to know that she had not suffered the same fate. But she was nowhere to be seen. He sat down between the two bodies, numb with shock and overcome by an intense bitterness at the futility of life. Strangely, he gave no thought to the perpetrator of this dreadful deed. There was no desire for revenge; only a desperate, pleading hope that she was unharmed.

For hours the young man sat there, the hot sun roasting his bronzed skin and the wind ruffling his fair hair, as it did the grey plumes of the ostrich behind him. For a long time no coherent thought came and he sat motionless as the vigilant vultures gathered overhead. They circled on silent wings, soaring in the hot air that rose off the desert. One, bolder than the rest, landed nearby, but the young man did nothing except to turn his head and stare blankly at it. With sinister patience, the bird squatted and stared back, waiting for him to leave so that it could begin its ghoulish task.

It was the wind that roused him – or, rather, the lack of wind as it stilled just before sunset. He stood and looked around at the ring of airborne undertakers who had landed and were waiting for the solitary mourner to depart. He gave them little thought, simply accepting them as one of the facts of life in this sterile place. They shuffled out of his way as he walked off and then rushed, squawking, upon their still, silent prey.

The young man did not look back. He continued walking, his eyes cast down, his mind deep in thought. He wondered if she knew what had happened and how he could find her.

Half a mile further on, he stopped abruptly and, walking back a few yards, bent to examine the ground. There, in the dust, were her footprints. To his experienced tracker's eye, it was immediately obvious that she had been running hard. The marks were deep and clear, their impression accentuated by the low angle of the setting sun. Again, his troubled mind turned somersaults as he set off in pursuit. He wondered if she too had been hurt, and slowed to examine the tracks for telltale signs of blood. There were none, but he felt little relief as he walked on, too tired now to run in the heat.

Darkness descended swiftly once the sun had set and he was no longer able to follow the tracks. Frustration boiled inside him as he stopped to rest, sinking wearily to sit on the ground. He felt thirsty. Slung over his shoulder, his water bottle contained four pints of warm, brackish water that had remained untouched throughout the long hot day. He began to take a long draught and then stopped himself in mid-swig, remembering that he had strayed quite some distance from his camp and that, until the sun came up again, he would not know in which direction to head. He must save some water for the morning. Food did not matter, as he had eaten that morning, but water was vital to survival, and he intended to survive.

With the onset of darkness, clouds gathered in readiness for the rain that should normally characterise this season of the year but which had been absent for the past four years of drought. Everyone had been praying that it would come again this year. Even if it did come, the longer-for rain seldom lasted a week, but even that slight watering would bring new growth and green to the arid grey landscape.

Rainfall on the escarpment far to the west could usually be relied upon to send brief torrents charging down one or two of the dry river beds, replenishing the underground stores that maintained the few wells in the region, but even that had failed to materialise for the last two years. It was all very well for those who lived in the mountains. At eleven thousand feet, the land was often shrouded in clouds and they were assured of water in all seasons, but it was very different down here.

The young man thought of these things for a while and hoped that the rain would not begin that night and wash out the tracks left by her flying feet. Then he remembered that the dawn wind would certainly remove them and he sighed heavily.

It was shortly afterwards that the thunderstorm had broken around him. Although violent, and bright with lightning, it brought no rain. Even so it crashed and thundered and bellowed like all the Bulls of Hades, echoing the turmoil of his mind. When it was over he lay down and dozed fitfully on the warm ground until the chill air woke him as the thin moon was setting and the dawn mist was beginning to form. He was wearing only shorts and a shirt and the cold seeped into him, causing him to wonder briefly whether he should return to camp instead of continuing his search. But his resolve returned with the warming rays of the early morning sun.

As soon as there was enough light to see by, he set off along the line of footprints, before the early breeze could obliterate them. The marks were closer now, indicating that she had slowed in her flight, and the impressions were less distinct where her feet had landed more gently. Once the wind started to get up the tracks quickly disappeared under a covering of dust, but he continued to follow their general direction. He walked most of the morning, following a vague line that might possibly have been tracks, turning aside now and then to examine patches of sparse scrub. Occasionally, he would scan the sky in case circling vultures might give him an unwelcome clue, but, much to his relief, the blue abyss remained empty.

Not long after the sun passed its zenith, he saw his tent a short distance away and realised that he must have walked in a huge circle; or had the tracks led him there? Could she have made for his camp, knowing that there would be safety and a friend? He searched all round for signs that she might have been in the vicinity, but found nothing. Later, as the sun sank towards the mountains in the west, he made another circle of the camp, using the low angle of the sun to highlight any slight trace of her presence there. It was at the same time of day, just before sunset, when he had seen her for the last time and had returned to his tent dejected at her going without acknowledging his call.

The following morning, he decided to go back to where he had found the body of her husband in the hope that she might have overcome her fear and returned to the scene. He took a spade and his water bottle and set off at a steady pace. He arrived to find that the undertakers had done their job well and rapidly. Little remained of either body apart from a scatter of bloody bones and a few feathers. Silently, he collected these and buried them in a pair of shallow graves, making a heap of soil over each and covering this with a layer of small stones collected from around the area. He offered no prayer for them; there was no point. No true God would have allowed this terrible thing to happen in the first place, so why now ask for the salvation of their souls?

Straightening up, he put the spade across his shoulders and draped his arms over it in the manner of a scarecrow. He made a wide circle, again looking for her tracks. There were none. She had not come back here. Sadly, he returned to camp and tried to think out a new plan for finding her. For the next four days he quartered the area from dawn to dusk without success.

On the fifth day, some of the people from the camp returned and rebuilt their domed grass huts. They had found enough grazing to last their herds for about two months and said that there was still some water beneath one of the wadis, only a few feet down.

The young man was glad to have their company as it softened his loneliness, but he could not talk about what had happened. The people knew that something was troubling him, but they did not ask. The following morning, work resumed and he threw himself into it with a vigour that made the others wonder. When they stopped at noon, he worked on alone in the scorching sun. He continued until it was too dark to see and then returned to his tent to brood.

The next day, just as work was due to end, two of the men came to him and asked him to go to their huts. One of the women had been bitten by a snake. When he heard what the problem was, he just nodded and laid down his shovel. Pausing only to pull a thorn from his foot, he collected his shirt and followed them without a word.

Someone had killed the snake and they showed it to him. Before looking at the woman, he took the snake and forced its mouth open with his thumb to expose the fangs. He examined them carefully for a few moments and then went to attend to the woman. She was young, about his own age, but very thin, and the venom was acting quickly. The bite was in her leg and may have hit a small blood vessel. With a piece of string from his pocket and a short stick from the ground, he made a rough tourniquet and applied it further up the leg. This should have been done sooner and he was anxious that too much time had been lost.

He stood up and issued a string of rapid instructions; someone to boil water, someone else to fetch a blanket to keep the woman warm, and the two men who had called him to run to his tent and bring him his small blue gas stove and red medicine box. They ambled off and he bellowed after them: "Run!" Being in English, the order would not have been understood, but something of his urgency must have got through, because they both broke into an unaccustomed trot. The young man turned back to the ring of silent watchers and asked quietly for someone to make tea for the woman.

The men returned with the red box and placed it on the ground beside the prostrate woman. From the box the young man took a rubber tube with which he replaced the string tourniquet. The patient moaned as he pulled it tight. Working rapidly, he selected an ampoule of serum, filled a syringe, and injected it into the vein at her elbow. It might have been better to have put it in behind her knee, closer to the source of the poison, but this was more accessible and he knew that speed must be the main priority in the circumstances.

The tea arrived and the woman's sisters propped her up and helped her to drink. Watched by a dozen pairs of dark brown eyes, his every movement observed in the most minute detail, the young man took a small enamel bowl from the box and filled it with spirit. From a polished steel container, he selected a surgical knife and a small curved needle, which he dropped into the spirit. The hot water arrived and he used it to wash his hands, rinsing them afterwards with more spirit. Not very sterile, but it would have to do. There was no time to be too fussy.

He swabbed the woman's leg with water and then spirit. Taking the knife, he made a deep cut some distance above the bite. The woman moaned again. Her blood flowed briefly and then stopped. He loosened the rubber tube to make it flow again and massaged her leg downwards to encourage the bleeding. He then wiped her leg again with spirit before placing his mouth over both wounds, sucking hard several times and spitting the foul tasting blood and venom onto the dusty ground. Then he retied the rubber tube.

With shaking hands, he threaded the curved needle with a length of bright blue silk and neatly sewed up the cut he had made. Next, he took a large dressing from the box, dusted it with antibiotic powder and bound it firmly over her leg before removing the rubber tube. He took the woman's wrist. She was unconscious now and her pulse was weak and fluttering. "We will know in an hour," he said quietly and sat back on his heels, still holding her wrist.

Someone handed him an old tin filled with treacly black tea. He looked up with a flicker of a smile as he took it, before looking back at the woman. He wondered if his effort had been wasted. Putting down the tea, he picked up the empty serum ampoule and inspected the label. It was out of date by some months and had not been kept cool, as instructed. Well, it was all there was and, anyway, he had been working on the fringes of his knowledge. There was little more he could do now beyond making her comfortable.

If the woman was strong enough she would recover, but nobody would blame him if she died. He knew that the people trusted him and that they knew that he had done what he could. If the worst happened, they would simply bury her, mourn briefly and quietly get on with their lives. He studied the woman again. She was one of those who used to bring him fresh goat's milk when all their herds had been here. "Please don't die," he spoke softly, in his own language. One of the men asked what he had said. "I was asking her not to die," he said.

Her pulse was still weak, but more regular now. He picked up the tin of tea with his free hand and drained it.

As he sat there holding the skinny hand, surrounded by those silent watchful people, he realised that for the last hour or so he had been concentrating so hard on what he was doing that it had pushed his former preoccupation right out of his mind. Now it all came flooding back to burden his thoughts again.

It was already getting dark, so he could not return to the release of hard physical work. He asked the men again about the grazing they had found and listened carefully as they told him in great detail. Soon, more people would return to work, they said.

Just before dawn, they came to him again to say that the woman was awake. He went to check on her. She was still very weak, but her pulse was even and much stronger and her eyes were alert. He changed the dressing, gave her husband some sugar and told him to make her drink plenty of sweet tea, then went back to his tent.

Some minutes later, the woman's daughter came and gave him an ostrich egg she had picked up in the desert the previous day. He asked her to stay and share it with him and she obediently knelt and blew life into the embers of his fire, adding small twigs and camel dung as she did so. The young man found a flat pan and some rancid sheep's butter, which he put on the fire to heat. As he broke the huge egg into the pan he saw again, with vivid clarity, the gruesome scene that had haunted his waking hours. The vision faded as he slowly stirred the egg and made an omelette.

That morning, he threw himself into the work with renewed energy, arousing more comment among his friends. He stopped twice to visit the woman. She was recovering well and was now sitting outside her hut. That evening, when he went to change the dressing, the woman's husband gave him a tin of thick tea and asked him obliquely why he was working so hard.

"The land has always been here and always will be. There is plenty of time for us to work," he said.

The fair-haired young man avoided meeting his eyes and stared moodily at the fire.

"The rain will come soon. If we are not ready, the water will be wasted," he said eventually, not wanting to think about it.

The man said there had been no rain for many years and would be none this year either. "That is the way of this place," he added.

They argued on for some time before lapsing into silence, both staring into the small dancing flames.

The man coughed. "The hunters came."

"I know," the young man replied. He took the nickel cartridge case from the pocket of his threadbare shorts and held it out. The man sucked his teeth noisily as he took it and turned it over in his fingers before the firelight. He marvelled at its brightness and thought enviously of the weapon that had fired it. He thought of his own rifle, which was older than his father and for which he had only three bullets.

"There are graves," he said eventually.

The young man met his eyes for the first time. "I made them. After you had gone to the grass," he replied and told his friend what had happened. When he had finished, the two men stared moodily into the fire again for a long time.

The older man threw a handful of dried dung onto the fire and the still evening air became heavy with the pungent aroma as it caught. He rose and brought more water to make tea, then squatted down on his heels again.

"She is of this place and knows its ways," he said after another pause. "She will be well."

The young man made no reply. His thoughts were with her, somewhere out there.

"She will come back," the man said, "when she wishes."

The next afternoon, several of the people stayed and worked with the young man until he stopped at sunset. And on the following day everyone stayed, unasked, and worked as long and as hard he did himself. After that, he gradually stopped earlier each day, realising that the people were already weakened by the drought and not driven by the same obsessive force that was pushing him on. He knew that they were now probably aware of what was behind his manic mood and were trying, in their own way, to ease his pain.

The days passed into weeks and, slowly, some measure of calm returned to the young man's mind. A new hope filled him; the man had told him she would come back. The old nomad knew this place, it was his home too. He also knew her and had predicted that she would come back.

Work on the project had been progressing rapidly, and the top half of the site was now completed. At least the people had something to show for their hard work, and if the rain came now and filled the dry river bed they would be able to plant a crop and the months of effort would be seen to have been worthwhile. The young man felt some measure of satisfaction at having achieved this with a group of nomads who had never done any organised work in the whole of their history.

The success of the project helped to put him in a more positive frame of mind and with no sign at all that the object of his obsession had stayed in the area after her husband's death, he had become sadly resigned to the likelihood that he would never see her again. He no longer spent hours combing the surrounding area in the hopes of catching a glimpse of her, although he couldn't help wondering from time to time what had become of her.

Then, one evening, an hour or so before sunset, he went out in search of firewood. He walked some distance from the encampment towards a slight rise covered with dead scrub. The sun had set and the light was fading fast when, quite unexpectedly, he came across some footprints. He knew immediately that they were hers, even before he bent to examine them. They were large and clear where they crossed a patch of soft soil on the gravel-strewn rise. There were only five prints, but few as they were, they spoke to him. She was still here!

He looked all around in the brief dusk, but could see nothing. Tomorrow he would find her. The thought flooded him with renewed hope. Near to where he stood there was an old broken anthill about five feet high. He scrambled up and stood on top of it to get a better view, but it was already too dark. He unslung his water bottle and placed it beside him as he settled down to watch and to wait.

"She will come back." The man's words echoed in his mind. Now she had come and was somewhere out there in the darkness. He wondered why it had never occurred to him to establish exactly where she lived. It no longer mattered. She had come back to him.

Once again, he sat through a long tropical night, oblivious to the raging of a storm around him. He thought over the events of the last few weeks. He remembered his fears for her when he had come across two bodies. He remembered his rising hope when he had found the signs that she had survived the attack and his disappointment at not being able to track her down. He remembered again the man's words, "She will come back." He had been given hope. "She is of this place and knows its ways. She will be well." He had been given reassurance. Fate could not be so cruel again.

Dawn exploded in a brilliant cascade of crimson across the eastern sky. The great fiery orb rose majestically into the heavens and flooded the desert with its warmth. The sky rapidly turned orange, and then golden as the sun climbed clear of the horizon. The mist, which had lain so dank and still after the storm, began to writhe and swirl as the first warm rays probed the barren earth. Soon it began to evaporate and within a few minutes it was gone. The empty sky became a dome of purest blue crystal and the cool air was clear and still. The sun's rays touched the young man's chilled skin and caressed him with their warmth. He stood up on top of the anthill and stretched.

Before too long, the air was in motion as the dawn breeze stirred. All manner of sounds now invaded the young man's consciousness. Nearby was an old acacia tree in which hundreds of yellow weaver birds tumbled and fluttered in noisy cacophony around the pendulous woven homes that dripped in profusion from the thin, flat-topped canopy. The jackal barked again in mournful farewell to another night of hunting. Its mate uttered a last howl of anguish at the sun that had so abruptly terminated their nocturnal revelry.

The young man turned, searching the desert around his vantage point. He raised his eyes to look further afield as he faced the sun once more.

That was when he saw her.

Silhouetted against the rising sun, she was standing beneath the one huge tree that rose from the empty plain like a statue suspended in time to dominate the landscape. She, too, was staring intently across the countryside. He could picture her calm face, with those curious marks like tear stains.

"She is looking for me. She knows I will come," he said, voicing the thoughts that were going through his mind. The sound of his own voice startled him and broke the moment.

Stiffly, he climbed down from the anthill and set off in her direction. He stopped and went back to pick up the water bottle, which had fallen to the ground unnoticed in the emotion of the dawn. He opened it and was about to drink when he lowered the bottle, replaced the cork and screwed on the metal cup. She may not have found water. He would save it for her. Again he set off, eyes fixed on the figure beneath the distant tree. A small sand lizard, basking in the early sunshine, scuttled out of his path unnoticed.

The young man's eyes were bright and there was now a spring in his step. The agonies that had haunted him for so long were banished and there was joy in his heart. The intervening distance dwindled rapidly as his long legs carried him ever closer.

The huge tree stood stark and gaunt against the sky as he approached. It was by far the tallest tree in this part of the desert and its size seemed the greater for its majestic isolation on a slight rise.

He saw that she was now lying down, watching his approach. She made no move to leave this time. She knew that he had come for her. She knew that he cared for her. When he was only a few yards from the tree, the young man halted, as if waiting for some sign that he should come closer. In silence, they looked into each other's eyes for several minutes, she lying in the shadow against the flaking bark of the tree, he standing tall and erect in the sun. His hair, flicked by the early wind, was the only movement.

The silence was broken by the haunting call of a hoopoe as it took wing from a nearby bush. Its pink body and black and white striped wings looked incongruous as its floppy, almost casual flight carried it away. They both watched it go and then they were alone. The young man turned to face her again. She looked different from the last time he had seen her, and he realised that she was heavily pregnant. He should have noticed before; it must have been evident for some time but he had not seen it.

Hesitantly, he walked forward. Her eyes followed every movement as he came. He sat down near her on the rough carpet of twigs and bark flakes. The sun was well up now and the thin canopy gave dappled shade that made attractive highlights on her skin. Slowly he reached out and brushed her shoulder lightly with his hand. She did not pull away, but continued to hold his eyes. Tenderly he let his fingers caress the soft curve of her neck. A shudder ran through her swollen body and she let out a soft moan.

With a shock, the young man became aware that she was not only pregnant but that her time had come. Still stroking her gently, he thought of the sadness that had brought him to this country. He thought of the recent events that had led up to this moment. They had both lost loved ones, but the closeness that now existed between them took away all that pain and he felt warm and whole again. He felt an overwhelming surge of affection for her.

The contractions were coming faster and her breathing rasped in the hot dry air. The young man opened his water bottle and filled the battered tin cup for her. She drank thirstily, clumsy in her haste, spilling much of the brackish water. He refilled the cup and she drank again before leaning back against the tree. He refilled the cup again and placed it on the ground beside her before putting the cork back in the water bottle. Her body shuddered again with another contraction.

The birth was quick and he lifted the sticky little body and placed it beside her heaving breast. The second came almost immediately and he lifted it and placed it with the first. Twins. That was good. She would not be alone again.

She gazed at her babies and then back at him, pride bright in her eyes. Her breathing was easier now and soon, with the delivery of the afterbirth, the spasms that had strained every sinew of her body subsided and ceased.

For a long time she lay and admired her babies. Then, as the sun warmed their tiny bodies, she rose and cleaned each one carefully before giving them suck.

Later, the young man left her and went in search of food. No words had passed between them but he knew that she understood, just as he did. He returned two hours before sunset with fresh water and meat. She drank thirstily again, but ate little. The young man could see from her nipples that she had been suckling her new children, and they looked full and contented.

As the sun dipped towards the mountains she got up and came to stand beside him where he sat. Together they remained, shoulder to shoulder, silently watching the perfect forms of the two new-born cheetahs as they slept in the warmth of the sun.

He put his hand on her shoulder and ran his fingers through the soft spotted fur of her long neck. She grunted softly and rubbed her beautiful sphinx head against his chest.

That night it rained in the desert for the first time in living memory.

Togo Telephone Tango

It should have been a very simple process.

The position of a telephone in our Togo office needed to be moved. The only vaguely complicating factor was that its new location was to be in the room next door, meaning not only that a longer cable would be required, but also that this cable would somehow have to reach the other side of the intervening wall.

Two obvious methods of accomplishing this immediately presented themselves. The cable could either follow the line of the wall, passing around the bottom of the doorway and along the other side until it reached the desired position in the other room; or it could pass directly through the intervening wall en route to its new location. Another, slightly more ambitious plan involved the possibility of the connecting wire being brought into the building next to the outer office window.

The first of these alternatives would require a great deal more cable, while the second would necessitate the drilling of a small hole through the dividing wall. The third would require the external wiring to be re-routed. On balance, the latter seemed the most sensible, but possibly the one most likely to produce problems since the original French engineers who had designed and built the city's telephone system were long gone and their local successors were not noted for their expertise in providing new lines.

We considered the matter for several days, mulling over the benefits of having the telephone installed in the outer office as against the advantages of leaving it in its present position. The possibility of having the telephone in the outer office, with an extension to the inner office was also discussed. This would require the purchase of two new instruments as well as all the new wiring, and would inevitably cost a great deal more. Eventually, the decision was made: the telephone would be moved to the outer office, which was always manned.

The Telecommunications Department was most helpful when I visited their office to arrange for the work to be carried out. Move the telephone? Yes, they could do that, it was part of their responsibility and nobody else was authorised to do anything to the telephone system. No, it was not a complicated job and would take very little time. Yes, they could do the job very soon; the engineer would come on Thursday. This was all most encouraging.

It didn't happen, of course. This being Africa, 'soon' is a relative term, open to very flexible interpretation. It actually took seven weeks and four more visits to the Telecommunications Department before the engineer arrived. To be fair, when he did turn up he came on the right day of the week.

Early one Thursday morning, a large dusty van drew up outside and five men tumbled out, looking like rejects from Dad's Army. They all trooped into the office and, without a word to anyone, began to search for the telephone. Once it had been located, they all inspected the instrument, lifting the handset and listening to it, peering into the microphone, and fiddling with the dial. Each one did this in turn and then set off to follow the wire to the point where it entered the building.

The proposed site for the instrument was inspected, then the wall between the two offices. With much nodding and scratching of heads the question of bypassing the wall was dissected.

They must have reached some kind of agreement, because one of the five then went and brought a bag of tools and a large reel of cable from the van. The other four piled into the van and drove off in a cloud of yellow dust.

In the outer office, the remaining functionary deposited his tools and the reel of cable in the centre of the floor and then stooped to examine the dividing wall at close quarters. After some time, he stood back to scratch his woolly head and surveyed the scene from a distance. With indecision written across his round face, he looked up and shrugged.

I knew there was a drainpipe embedded in the dividing wall some four inches along from where it joined the outside wall. It occurred to me that I should make the fact known to this man, just in case. I told him about the pipe and showed him where it was hidden in the wall. He nodded knowingly, pointing to the wall with a chisel and muttering: "Égout. Égout dans le mur."

With a thick pencil, I marked a small cross on the wall and suggested that this would be a good place for him to make the hole he was contemplating. His bobbing head signified agreement and, pointing to the cross, he displayed a toothless set of pink gums and said that it was indeed a very good place for the hole. Encouraged by the man's obvious common sense, I left him to get on with the job.

Big mistake!

The telephone engineer, for that is what he claimed to be, put down the chisel that he had been brandishing, bent himself double and proceeded to scrabble about inside his voluminous tool bag. This process was accompanied by a series of clanks from within the bag and grunts from the man when his oversized jacket slipped over his inverted shoulders and engulfed his head in its folds. Various items were ejected from the bag to clatter onto the polished stone floor as the clanking and grunting increased in intensity. The performance prompted visions of the mating ritual of a mechanical excavator!

At last the jacket was shrugged back to its proper position as the noble fellow emerged triumphant from the tool bag, clutching a large lump hammer. He then had to search the debris on the floor to relocate the chisel he had deposited there whilst searching for the hammer. He found it and was now ready to proceed. He advanced on the wall and attacked it with gusto.

It might have been better to have used some form of drill, but the engineer exuded confidence as though he did this sort of thing every day and was a real expert. He seemed to be doing quite a neat job. At least, it seemed so until the chisel came through the other side of the wall where it burst out, carrying with it a piece of masonry the size of a large dinner plate.

As the chisel disappeared into the wall, the engineer stood back to admire his achievement, looking suitably pleased with himself. Indeed, he had every reason to be pleased if one only looked at the entry point. He moved through the doorway to examine the other side. His face registered mild surprise when he saw the crater he had made and the scatter of smashed plaster and masonry on the floor. His hand went up, in the now familiar gesture, and scratched his head.

It would be simple enough to repair, I was informed, and the engineer would even see that it was repainted. Only at this point did I notice that he had not made the hole in the spot that we had agreed, but right where the drainpipe descended in the wall cavity. Still, there did not appear to be any serious damage.

Now began the job of extending the cable. This proved to be no simple task and took some time. First the engineer measured the wall. Then he measured the length of cable and cut it from the reel. He stripped off the outer insulation from the first foot of wire before securing it to the wall next to where the repositioned telephone was to stand. Working his way towards the newly made hole in the dividing wall, he used clips to attach the cable to the plaster at regular intervals until he was able to feed it through the hole. He then went into the other room.

The floor was still littered with the debris of his excavation, which crunched under the engineer's sandal shod feet as he approached the hole. He grasped the end of the cable and pulled the slack through. Using more cable clips he led this along the wall in the direction of the original entry wire, fixing it firmly as he moved forward. He reached the end only to find that it was at least a metre too short.

The engineer stood back to survey the problem and scratched his head. He returned to the first room and traced his work back from the beginning, scratching all the way, the look of puzzlement on his face growing all the way back to the where the cable fell just too short. With a look of resignation, he shrugged and began removing the new cable from the wall, leaving a neat line of craters where the clips had pulled the plaster away.

Having roughly stripped the cable away, the engineer returned to his reel and peeled the outer insulation from the first foot to reveal the technicolor vermicelli within. Then, using the first cable as a guide, he measured off a new length, adding two yards for good measure before cutting it from the reel. Unhurriedly, he proceeded as before, attaching the new cable with yet more clips, spaced between the craters where the first set had been removed.

This cable was also a yard too short! The engineer raked vigorously at his well-clawed scalp again. I wondered if he had lice. Perhaps he had got the two cables mixed up and had reinstalled the first one? No, that one was too short. He had added extra to this one to make sure it was long enough. He waved his arms as he explained.

The second cable was removed from the wall, doubling the number of little craters in the plaster. The engineer coiled up the two lengths of cable, took out his cutters and clipped a yard from the end of each one. This done he disappeared out of the door with the two short pieces.

When he came back five minutes later things really began to go with a swing. Picking up the reel of cable, he fed the free end through the wall. Skipping round to the other side he took the free end and pulled it along to the junction box. With great care he stripped the end and made the connections. This done he sat back on his haunches to survey the job and once more attacked his scalp.

Grunting with approval, he now began to work his way along the cable, fixing it to the wall carefully so as to hide as much of the evidence of the two previous attempts as possible. In the outer office, when he came to the position where the telephone was to be installed, he cut off an extra ten feet of cable. From this he began carefully to strip the outer insulation, exposing the brightly coloured filaments within.

Very carefully, he connected the ends to the instrument and then bundled up the surplus length into an untidy rainbow bird's nest. He lifted the receiver and held it to his ear. It buzzed comfortingly. He was not a telephone engineer for nothing!

At this point things became even more interesting. Someone in the apartment above the office decided to empty the bath. A brief gurgling sound from the hole in the wall turned every eye in that direction in time to see a flood of dirty, scummy, foaming water pour out onto the office floor. In a matter of seconds the flood covered the floor in both offices and the telephone engineer was scampering about trying to rescue the tools he had previously strewn about with such casual abandon. He showed little surprise at the flood and made no move to do anything about either stopping it or clearing up the mess. He stuffed the tools into his bag and heaved it out of the open doorway. Pausing only to check that the telephone still had a dialing tone, he announced that someone would be along very soon to mend the wall, then vanished in pursuit of his tool bag before anyone could say anything.

I telephoned the department responsible and asked to speak to the boss. He was out. They made a note of the matter and assured me that someone would come round without delay to put things right. Some chance, I thought, and decided to call again later. My decision, however, had been hasty. Within a few minutes the dusty green van screeched to a halt outside and the original team of five, including the engineer, tumbled out and trooped into the office to inspect the scene.

They all gazed in awe at the flood before gingerly stalking forward to inspect its source. The hole in the wall elicited a great deal of head shaking, scalp scratching and excited chatter. Both sides of the wall were inspected, and each man lifted the handset and checked that the telephone still appeared to be functioning.

After some further discussion, they all agreed that the drain pipe was broken but added that they could do nothing about it since they did not have the correct materials with them. Someone would be along first thing in the morning to make the repair. Could we avoid letting any more water out until then? I tried to explain that the apartment above was nothing to do with us, but it was no use. Like Snow White's dwarfs, the whole team marched out in line, climbed into their van and roared off in another cloud of yellow dust.

Tomorrow meant next week if I was lucky, I thought, and telephoned the Department again. The boss was still out and would not be back that day. Yes, they knew all about the hole; I had already told them. They had it on the list and someone would come and fix it as soon as possible.

But the office floor was flooded, weren't they going to do something about that? When the men came to fix the hole they would see to that as well, so please not to let any more baths out. It was useless trying to explain. Meanwhile, the foul smell was beginning to provoke a new line of worry. Did the pipe merely carry bath water or was it also the sewer? I told the voice on the other end of the 'phone about this new concern. As soon as possible, I was assured and the dialing tone filled my ear.

I went upstairs to explain the problem to the people in the apartment above and to ask if it would be possible not to let out any more water. There was nobody there. I scribbled a note and pushed it under the door.

True to their promise, and much to my surprise, the Dad's Army squad returned the next morning, arriving in their battered green van wreathed in smiles and yellow dust. They once again trooped into the office in line and each in turn inspected the hole in the wall and the stain on the floor where the flood had been before lifting the handset to see that the telephone was still working. Accompanied by the habitual head scratching and nodding, the group then held a muttered conference.

Tools were produced and the engineer began to disconnect the cable he had installed the previous day, stripping it from the wall to make yet another line of craters where the clips were pulled out. As the cable was pulled through the hole in the wall, another man produced a large hammer and chisel, which he wielded with devastating effectiveness to enlarge the crater, starting at the point where I had marked a cross the previous morning.

The hammer thumped, the chisel clanged and the masonry flew, littering the office floor with gritty shards. Within a few minutes, the hole had been enlarged until there was a two foot square opening and the damaged drain pipe was exposed. The whole gang now inspected the new hole and another muttered conference was held.

They evidently decided that the hole was still too small, because the demolition specialist resumed his onslaught only to find that the bookcase was in the way. Would I please move it? No, I would not, but they were welcome to do so themselves, provided that the papers and books were not disarranged. The man who had asked tried lifting one end. It was heavy and he did not look too keen.

He tried the other end. It was just as heavy and he looked slightly forlorn. Heads were scratched again as he appealed to the chisel man to do his work without moving the furniture.

This he flatly refused to do, and after a few minutes hesitation they decided that a team effort was required. With two men on each end, the bookcase was dragged screeching and creaking across the floor to be abandoned in the centre of the room. The chisel man, who had not participated in this strenuous activity, attacked the wall again, more gently this time.

After ten minutes' chipping, he peered into the cavity, grunted with satisfaction and announced that there was a hole in the drainpipe! I wondered why he had come. The rest of the gang joined the inspection, nodding wisely and confirming that there was indeed a hole in the drainpipe. They all looked at one another with pleased expressions on their faces.

The telephone engineer reattached his cable, fed it through the enlarged hole and clipped it neatly to the wall. Having made the reconnection, he stood back to admire his handiwork, stepped on the plastic cover of the junction box and crushed it. He looked contrite and went to check that the telephone was once again in order. It purred comfortably as he lifted the handset, and he looked much happier.

Meanwhile, the rest of the gang were mixing cement on a board just outside the front door and importing a selection of broken concrete blocks and scraps of tin. The demolition expert was also a reconstruction specialist, it seemed. He fashioned a very neat patch out of one of the tin scraps, fitted it to the broken pipe with some sticky yellow paste to make the seal and then wired it firmly in place.

As the engineer finished fixing his fourth set of cable clips, the masons began on the wall. In a matter of minutes, they had the hole filled and were plastering mortar over the repaired surface. It was special waterproof mortar, they told me proudly, just to make sure there were no more leaks. When they had finished both sides, there was a small amount of the special mortar left over. The engineer took this and a small trowel and made a very neat job of filling in the innumerable craters he had made elsewhere in the walls.

The finished job looked very presentable, all things considered, and the telephone still worked. With happy chatter, the gang cleared up the debris and swept the floor. They collected their tools, said they'd be back and vanished in the customary swirl of yellow dust, leaving the bookcase standing in the centre of the outer office. Lifting the phone to ring the department and grumble at this, I looked at the huge wet cement patch on the stark whiteness of the wall. The lines of small grey dots made it seem as if the office had been machine-gunned. I realised the whole lot would need painting and it had, therefore, been sensible enough to leave the furniture away from the wall. Maybe they would come back as they'd promised. They had before. I replaced the handset.

On Saturday morning, I went into the office with the expectation of having some peace and quiet to catch up on all my paperwork after the disruptions of the previous two days. Within minutes of my starting work there was a squeal of brakes outside, a slamming vehicle door, voices and the sound of footsteps coming across the courtyard. The office door was flung open and the telephone engineer marched in, followed by the rest of his gang.

With a brief nod to me, they inspected the previous day's work, tested the telephone and, of course, scratched their heads while they discussed the job. Look, test, scratch, talk; the routine was familiar by this time. The cement had dried and looked less obtrusive now, but they were not satisfied. It would have to be painted, they told me. When? Now! And they all trooped out to the van again.

Two men returned with paint brushes, another with a large can of paint and a fourth brought a bundle of cloth that he spread over the floor to catch any drips and splashes. The engineer stood watching, a satisfied smile on his face. The grey cement scar was rapidly covered with new paint. They even remembered the line of repaired holes along the cable's length. I was impressed.

Within half an hour, the job was done. They collected their brushes, paint and cloths, checked the telephone again and, with toothy grins all round, piled into their van and drove away. I went to the gate to see them off and watched until their van disappeared round the corner before going back into the office.

The bookcase still stood in the middle of the room. The walls were stark and white. The new paint was bright green!

I picked up the telephone to ring the local hardware store and order some white paint. There was no comforting buzz. The line was dead.

Bones of Contention

The village granaries were tall conical structures with an aperture at the top large enough for a small boy to climb through. They were built of mud blocks on a wooden base, raised a foot off the ground to prevent rats and damp from entering, and plastered inside and out with clay. Once full, a wooden plug was put in the top, sealed with more clay and a thatched hat added to keep the rain off.

Harvest was a time when the whole village worked from dawn until dusk. In the fields, the men cut down the tall sorghum plants, stripping the leaves to save as feed for their few animals and stacking the canes to be used for fencing or as building materials. The heavy, loose grain heads were piled into baskets.

Chattering and laughing, a constant stream of women and girls would then lift the laden baskets onto their heads and march in stately procession from the fields to the village. Here, under the watchful supervision of those too old for manual labour, the young boys would load the grain into the waiting granaries. The whole process would be accompanied throughout by gossip, laughter and rhythmic songs that helped to maintain the steady pace of the work.

After ten days of this communal labour, the final field was cleared and the last granary was filled. Throughout the afternoon the Wa-Wa man – the village witch doctor – had been touring the granaries, casting his spells and uttering incantations as the tops were sealed and the thatched hats hoisted into place.

Each family paid for this service with baskets of grain that were carefully loaded into the Wa-Wa's own granary. He was the only man in the village who had no fields and grew no crops of his own. Even so, the community ensured that he never went hungry, even when they did themselves, for he was viewed with a mixture of fear and venerable respect. Later that day, he would cast bones and read his oracle to predict the coming of the brief winter rains that would allow the fields to be tilled for a quick crop of vegetables.

By dusk, everything was done. The granaries were all sealed and their hats were in place. All had been blessed by the Wa-Wa and the last men had returned from the fields. A thin pall of wood smoke, fed by a hundred cooking fires, lay over the village in a lazy grey blanket on the still evening air. Smells of cooking mingled with the pungent tang of the smoke as the women busied themselves preparing the evening meal. Groups of men sat in their compounds, talking quietly while the evening chorus of crickets scraped out an incessant shrill buzz to accompany the soft rhythm of a drum that rippled through the gathering darkness from somewhere on the far side of the village.

This balmy peace was suddenly shattered by the sharp yelp of a dog and the anguished screech of a man's voice. This was followed by a stream of savage curses from near the edge of the village. The voice that uttered these imprecations grew louder and more agitated with every passing second. Men abandoned their discussions and went to seek out the source of the disturbance. I lifted my cooking pot from the fire and followed them.

As we approached, the stream of invective became even more strident and more violent. I wondered what foul crime had been committed to cause such outrage, and by whom. Disturbances of this sort were rare in the village. Loud arguments were not unknown, but they usually subsided quite quickly and had little anger in them. This was something quite different.

Following the noise to its source, I found that a large crowd of curious people had already gathered. Whilst outwardly many people showed signs of alarm at the incident, some of the younger ones were hiding smiles behind their hands and exchanging whispered comments of derision as they watched the scene before them.

The source of the commotion turned out to be the Wa-Wa man, who was leaping about in front of his newly filled granary, brandishing a heavy stick and yelling at the top of his voice. Much of what he said was unintelligible and presumably involved mystical phrases known only to the initiated. Whatever it was, it sounded ferocious. I wondered for a moment if he was simply dissatisfied with the tithe the villagers had paid him, but this was evidently not what had upset him.

From time to time he would stop leaping about to lunge with his stick and thrash about beneath the granary. Then his frenzied gyrations would be resumed as, with intense passion, he called down every imaginable evil on whatever unfortunate creature was cowering beneath the structure.

I pushed forward in order to get a better view. As I reached the front of the crowd, the Wa-Wa made a huge leap and then spun round and froze. Pointing at me with his stick, he screamed: "You! You have done this! I shall beat you and drive out the evil spirit that has inhabited you!" And with that, he lunged forward to jab me with his stick.

With the press of bodies from behind, I could not move smartly enough to avoid a painful blow in the middle of my chest. He was a wizened little man, almost a hunchback, but surprisingly strong and remarkably agile. He was adept at wielding a stick to painful effect.

His next blow was aimed at my head and I just managed to grab the stick and hold on to it, even though it stung my hands as though it were red hot. I twisted sharply and managed to wrench the weapon from his grasp. The crowd gasped. It was unheard of to challenge the Wa-Wa like this.

In the stunned silence that followed I realised why his blow had stung my hands so much. The stick was on fire and I had grabbed the burning end! I threw it down and put my foot on it to stop him snatching it back.

"What is it that is my fault?" I demanded. "And why are you attacking me with a burning stick?" Some of the steam seemed to go out of the Wa-Wa man, but he still scuttled angrily back and forth in front of his granary.

"You have brought all these new things to the village!" he yelled at me. "Grain that has white seeds, peppers that have no fire in them, roots that grow fat and orange and strange plants that have big black fruits. What are these things?"

"But..." I started.

"You make donkeys to dig the fields and boxes to take the colour out of the water. And you talk to dogs!" With this, he turned and again started attacking the space under his granary.

"What is the problem that has upset you?" I shouted back at him.

Again there was an audible gasp from the now otherwise silent crowd. Nobody had ever dared argue with the Wa-Wa man, let alone shout at him. He is a powerful man who can do magical and mysterious things. He can see beyond where mortal men can see. The Wa-Wa man should be revered, respected, feared and obeyed. It was dangerous to challenge or anger him and I, evidently, had just done both.

"That dog you talk to," he yelled in aggrieved tone, "it has stolen my *gurri*. You told it to do that and now it is there!" He pointed under the granary. "Why do you make it steal my *gurri*?" He was almost crying with frustration.

I had no idea what a *gurri* might be and had certainly not told any dog to take it. Whatever a *gurri* was, the offending dog had evidently taken refuge under the granary when the Wa-Wa man tried to get it back.

"What dog?" I asked, quietly. "And what is this *gurri* that it has taken?"

"My *gurri*!" he wailed, wringing his hands. "It has taken my *gurri* and will eat it!"

"Where is the dog?"

"There!" he pointed to the space below his granary. "You must talk to it and make it give my *gurri* back!"

I bent down to have a look. It was almost dark now and the space beneath the granary was pitch black. Someone passed a lantern to me and I saw a pair of bright eyes reflected in the dim light. Moving closer, I could see a small tan and white shape cowering in the darkness and looking extremely frightened. In its mouth was something dark and knobbly.

I recognised the dog. It was only a puppy, really. There were five or six dogs that lived around the village. Nobody seemed to own them and nobody gave them any attention, except me. I had managed to make friends with all except one and they would usually come when I whistled. This little fellow was normally very friendly and playful.

I got down on my belly and started to make friendly noises as I moved closer. The tip of the dog's tail twitched nervously. As I reached out towards the frightened dog, the Wa-Wa man again lunged into the space with his stick and resumed his litany of curses. I snatched the stick from him again, rolled away and got to my feet.

"What are you doing?" I shouted at him. "Do you want that dog to come out? All you are doing at the moment is making him more afraid and that will only ensure that he stays where he is."

"I want my *gurri*!" wailed the Wa-Wa man.

"Then be quiet and let me see if I can get him to come out," I said angrily.

The crowd began to murmur, and I realised that this situation could turn nasty if I was not careful. It would not do for the Wa-Wa man to lose face in front of his villagers. If something were not done to restore his dignity there could be trouble.

I went back to coaxing the dog and started all over again with soft words and slow movements. After a few minutes, the animal leaned forward and sniffed at my hand. Finding someone familiar and friendly, it dropped the object it held in its mouth and began to lick my fingers. I started stroking its muzzle in return.

The object the dog had been holding in his jaws rolled towards me as soon as he dropped it. With my free hand, I picked it up and pushed it down the front of my shirt. I petted the dog and talked quietly to it for several minutes before slowly backing out of the confined space.

Gradually, the dog gained confidence and crawled after me. As soon as I got clear and could sit up, I scooped the animal into my arms and climbed to my feet. There was a ripple of hushed comment from the crowd as I held the animal in front of me. Its mouth was open, tongue lolling, and its skinny belly was exposed for everyone to see.

"It has eaten my *gurri*!" the Wa-Wa man wailed again.

"No, it hasn't," I said. "It has eaten nothing for a long time. See how skinny it is. But it dropped something under the granary."

The Wa-Wa man seized the lantern and got down to peer into the dark space. Still holding onto the dog, I edged round the side of the granary as the press of villagers moved forward to see what the Wa-Wa man would retrieve.

Within moments, I found myself on the outer edge of the crowd, so I turned and walked quietly away. Behind the granary was an open space where the Wa-Wa man performed many of his rituals. On the ground lay the skin that he used for divination, covered with a scattering of the old blackened bones that featured in these rituals.

Like Saul on the road to Tarsus, I suddenly saw the light and understood exactly what must have happened. The Wa-Wa man had been casting the bones of his oracle to foretell the coming rains. The movement and rolling bones had been too much of a temptation for a playful puppy, particularly a hungry one. As the bones were tossed onto the skin, the dog must have snatched one and run off with it, taking refuge under the granary when the Wa-Wa man gave chase.

Reaching into my shirt, I pulled out the knobbly object that the dog had had in its mouth. It was a large round neck vertebra, stained dark with age and polished smooth with handling. I surreptitiously dropped it on the skin, without looking round, and carried the dog back to my own compound. The Wa-Wa man was still poking around under his granary, but the main part of the excitement was obviously over. People were drifting away, back to their supper, and I did the same.

Not long after this, there was another brief outburst of excited shouts from the direction of the Wa-Wa man's house. Moments later, I heard my neighbour, Birrim, coming back and called over the wall to ask what the new excitement was about.

"There was nothing under the granary, but he found the *gurri* where he had thrown it with the other bones," Birrim, told me.

"That's good," I said. "Maybe now he will not beat the dog."

"No, but he will be angry with you for shouting at him. He must punish you for that."

"He has already burned my hands with that stick of his," I protested, aware once more of the stinging in my palms.

"Such things happen when the Wa-Wa is upset," said Birrim, with resignation, from beyond the wall.

There was music and drumming and dancing in the village that night and I went along with Birrim and joined in. Despite the events of the early evening, I still seemed to be welcome among the villagers and was greeted with the usual teasing and smiles. Nobody seemed displeased or uncomfortable at my presence, and my earlier apprehension vanished.

The party went on long into the night. The drumming was vibrant and the dancing energetic. The musicians and drummers worked in relays to maintain the momentum of the party. Bowls of *dolo*, a millet beer brewed in the village, were passed round and everyone got slightly drunk. I finally staggered back to my own house, happy and tired, at about 3.30 a.m.

The dog, to whom I had fed part of my own supper, was still curled up in the corner of the courtyard. As I came in he opened one eye and the tip of his tail twitched briefly before he subsided once more into a contented slumber.

A few minutes later, I was just getting ready for sleep myself when there was a scratching at the courtyard door. When I opened it, the Wa-Wa man scuttled in furtively and quickly pushed the door closed behind him. The dog opened a wary eye and watched him.

"My *gurri* is returned," he announced in a whisper, before thrusting a small leaf-wrapped package into my hand. "That is medicine for your burned hands."

"Thank you. But what is this *gurri* that you had lost?" I asked, not sure if he would tell me.

"It was my grandfather's," he said. "It is important for my oracle to see clearly. *Gurri* gives the vision, and tonight it had great power."

"Did your grandfather give it to you, then?" I, too, was whispering.

"How could he? It was his. After the French colons killed him, my father took it, and then gave it to me when I was initiated."

Realisation dawned. The bone that I had held earlier had been the top vertebra from his grandfather's neck. No wonder it was precious to him. I sincerely hoped that the dog had not chewed it or damaged it in any way.

"When I saw my *gurri* again tonight it had cast a powerful vision and the oracle was as clear as I have ever seen before." He was gripping my arm and his whisper was conspiratorial as he stared into my face.

"But why are you telling me like this, secretly, in the middle of the night?" I asked.

"Because of what happened today and what the oracle told me. I was angry with you because the dogs like you and one of them had taken my *gurri*. I was angry because of all the new things that have come to the village since you made your house here. Tonight, the oracle showed me that these are good things that you have done for our people and we should be thankful for them. I have said angry things. What I said before I must now unsay."

This! From a witch doctor? It was unheard of. I was stunned.

"But I shouted and was rude to you. This cannot be, or the people will lose their belief," I whispered back. "You are the Wa-Wa. Nobody may challenge you with impunity."

"So what should I do?" he asked. "I have already burned your hands. That is punishment and the people have seen this."

"But it was not declared publicly as a punishment. That will still need to be done if they are to believe," I said.

"They will believe. Not everything the Wa-Wa does needs clear explanation. If they understood everything they would have no need of me and mine. What they need is the mysteries I make." His tone was conspiratorial.

"Then I shall give you a mystery for them. Sit and I will show you," I said, pushing him towards a large log that served as a seat.

He released my arm and sat down. I went into the house and returned with two bottles of beer and a packet of seeds. His eyes lit up when he saw the beer. Bottled beer was a treat in this isolated place.

"Tomorrow I shall plant some more vegetables," I explained. "First some small plants that I have already started growing and then some seeds. When I start to plant the seeds you can put a curse on them." I explained the idea that had suddenly come to me, telling him in some detail exactly what form the curse should take.

There was a delighted look of pure mischief on his face as I spoke and I hoped he could not really cast such a spell. I had no doubt of the truth of his powers, but with luck he would not actually be able to do what I had just described.

"Can this be so?" he asked with quiet wonder.

"You are the Wa-Wa. If you say it is so, then it will be so," I said, hoping he had never seen these seeds before. I opened the beer and he drank it with relish.

The villagers were always curious about my horticultural activities, so there was an audience of more than a dozen people later that morning when I planted out five rows of tomato and pepper seedlings. When the little plants were watered in, I raked over a new line of soil and planted a row of seeds.

The Wa-Wa man chose that moment to arrive. With a rattling of bones and clanking of the iron bells with which he bedecked himself, he materialised with a suddenness that startled everyone, me included. He at once began to dance up and down the rows of newly planted seedlings, muttering and chanting. He stopped and peered at some of the plants before moving on.

Mocking me as the man who talks to dogs and donkeys, he began to berate me for shouting at him the previous evening. He was eloquent and elaborate in his descriptions and it really impressed the watching villagers. It impressed me, too. Finally, he called down punishment for my misdemeanours and cursed the seeds I had just planted and the plants that would grow from them. He said that their roots would be deformed and grow fat; when I harvested my crop it would cry out in pain and drip blood on the ground. My white hands would turn red and be covered in that blood. If I ate the crop it would foul my insides, and the same day I would pass blood instead of water.

This was quite a punishment and it had been delivered with the full drama of an accomplished performer. As his tirade reached a climax, he hurled the object that he had been waving about onto the ground on top of the line of seeds. I just had time to notice that it was a rib bone before a swift black and brown body dashed forward, snatched the bone and ran off.

The Wa-Wa man let out a howl of rage. Tearing a heavy iron bell from the thong around his neck, he hurled it after the fleeing dog. A stream of foul language followed the bell to its mark. There was a clank and the dog yelped. It dropped the bone and disappeared into some bushes. The Wa-Wa man scuttled over and retrieved his bone and the bell.

"More trouble with your *gurri*?" I asked as he came back.

"No, this is *inayenyii*," he cried indignantly, holding up the bone. "It was my grandmother's!"

Once again, I could understand why he did not want it chewed by a village cur. Apart from that, the sight of dogs continually running off with sacred bones was not doing the Wa-Wa man's image much good. I hoped the outcome of his earlier performance would redress the balance.

The offending dog was not seen around the village for more than a week. When at last it did appear, its tail had a sharp kink half way down. The Wa-Wa's bell had been heavy and had clearly found its mark. People marvelled when they saw this further manifestation of his power and I received many a sideways glance and speculative enquiry about the health of my vegetable patch.

The Wa-Wa's credibility was beyond dispute a couple of months later when I announced that I was going to harvest some of the vegetables I had been planting the day the dog stole the Wa-Wa's *inayenyii*. By the time I reached the vegetable garden, there was quite a gathering of people who had come to see how my crop had done.

They admired the tomatoes that were large and firm and were clearly impressed by the size of the green peppers. Favourable comments were also passed on the okra and the melons. Everyone wanted to see and handle the produce to assure themselves that things were as they should be. But when I eventually moved towards the spot where the Wa-Wa had hurled his bone to the ground, a hush descended.

I took my trowel and dug into the ground at the base of a plant. The trowel scraped on a stone, making a short screech, and there was a sharp intake of breath. I reached down, grabbed the plant by the roots and squeezed as I lifted it. The people stared aghast as the juice dripped dark and red onto the pale soil and spread in bloody smears across my palms.

They stepped back in awe as I showed them my crop. Then they remembered the Wa-Wa's curse and several women ran off shrieking. The offender had been punished, exactly as the Wa-Wa had said. His power could not be doubted.

People turned away to go and discuss this extraordinary event. And I took my beetroot home for lunch.

Arnie's Wives

The seventy or so houses surrounding the communal space in the centre of the village were wrapped in a tall stockade of poles and cane fencing. Some of the poles had been freshly cut when the stockade was built and had then sprouted to grow bushy crowns of leaves that effectively disguised the village in the wooded countryside. Small fields of maize, millet and manioc were scattered over a wide area in clearings around the village. Closer to the stockade a number of small vegetable plots produced yams, peppers and tomatoes.

Nestling in the foothills of Mount Elele, the village of Amèzod-jikopé was one of the larger settlements in the Assouakoko Forest Reserve, with a population of about three hundred. The modern world had hardly touched these people, who earned their subsistence by cultivating a few fields, gathering fruits and honey, and by hunting in the surrounding forest. Apart from some brightly coloured cloth and a few tools, which had to be brought in from the nearest town, the community was completely self sufficient.

I was quite surprised, therefore, when I received a message from the village headman asking for help. The message was addressed to me by name, despite the fact that I had never visited the area before, and, apart from anything else, I was interested to know how he had obtained this information. It was thus with considerable curiosity that I set off on what was to be the first of numerous happy visits to Amèzodjikopé.

The road ended seven kilometres beyond Kouniohou. From there it degenerated into a rough track, twisting and turning through the undulating forest. No vehicle had passed that way for a long time and it was necessary to use low ratio four-wheel drive for much of the journey. I crawled for nearly six hours to cover the final thirty-eight kilometres, stopping from time to time to clear rocks and fallen logs from the track. At last, I came over a rise and, through a gap in the trees, saw smoke drifting upwards from a clearing in the forest below.

It was late afternoon when I reached Amèzodjikopé and as I pulled up outside the stockade my Landrover was immediately surrounded by a milling crowd of smiling, curious children. Some of the older ones called out "Ambeke" (welcome), whilst the youngest simply stood and stared with open mouths. As I heaved my aching limbs out of the driving seat, the crowd was already starting to swell rapidly with the arrival of the adults.

A tall man, standing head and shoulders above the rest, eased his way towards me, gently laying his hands on the shoulders of those in front of him to seek free passage. People moved aside and made way for him as he approached me with outstretched hands,

"I am Djégoumana. Welcome to Amèzodjikopé," he announced in excellent French, shaking my hand with a firm but surprisingly gentle grasp. "You may leave the car there. It will not be touched."

He led me into the village. People reached out to touch me or to shake my hand as we passed, saying "Ambeke," as they did so. The crowd followed as the headman led me towards a mud-walled house at the side of the central clearing. The house had recently been re-thatched and looked fresh and tidy. A thick grass mat, new and green, lay on the ground outside the doorway. The headman motioned towards this, inviting me to sit.

Djégoumana's age was difficult to define. His thick hair and sparse beard were touched in places by grey, but this was the only indication. His skin was a rich chocolate and his hands were remarkably smooth compared to those of the other villagers, which were coarse and callused by hard work. He also had unusually long, delicate fingers. His face was criss-crossed by an intricate pattern of finely cut tribal scars that gave depth to his features and emphasis to the wisdom in his dark brown eyes. He was a dignified man, with an aura of calm authority and he was treated with obvious respect by everyone.

As soon as we were seated, a young woman approached and offered a calabash of fresh palm wine. The headman nodded his acceptance, raising the bowl towards me in salutation and then drinking from it before passing it to me. I repeated the gesture, taking a swig and then passing the bowl back. Others joined us and the palm wine circulated. Corncobs, freshly toasted on a charcoal brazier, were brought and the palm wine calabash was refilled.

Over the next couple of hours, Djégoumana told me about his village and the problem that had caused him to summon me. He also explained how he had known my name.

For some time, people had been falling sick in the village and a number of cases had been quite serious. Nobody had actually died until recently, when there had been three fatalities in rapid succession. The village medicine woman had tried her best with the traditional herbal remedies, but to no avail. Nobody was certain what caused the sickness, but the headman was unwilling to place the blame purely on malevolent spirits.

There was an old French monk who occasionally travelled round the villages. Although he was based at the monastery near Dzogbegan, a week's hard walk to the south, he was a medical monk, not a religious missionary. Most of the people in this region were animists and spurned any religion that did not recognise their spirits and deities. The old monk, however, was welcome everywhere, despite his affiliation.

On his latest visit to Amèzodjikopé he had found a dozen or more people suffering from fevers and severe stomach problems. He treated them and then spent a couple of days looking into the matter in an effort to trace the cause. Finally, he decided that the problem originated in the water supply and advised Djégoumana of this.

There was no well in the village, so the women were obliged to walk several kilometres to collect water from a stream every morning. They then had to walk back, carrying the heavy burden on their heads. The stream had become contaminated and now ran red and foul and as the few springs nearby gave very little water, the women were having to walk almost three times as far, often on steep paths, to fetch the daily water. This activity now took up so much of their time that there was not enough for working in the fields and collecting from the forest. People were already going thirsty. Now they were getting hungry as well.

It was the itinerant monk who had told Djégoumana about me, giving him my name and suggesting that he should contact me for assistance. He had apparently heard about me further north, in the area where I had recently been working. The headman could not write, so the monk agreed to do this for him, and one of the villagers had then walked two days to Kouniohou, the nearest Post Office, to send the letter. So, here I was.

The next morning, I was taken on a tour of the village. Djégoumana and a number of the villagers showed me the local springs and the polluted stream. It was easy to see the problem, but not what had caused it. And although the solution would probably be fairly simple, it would take time to carry out the necessary work properly and someone would be needed on site all the time to supervise the operation.

I explained this to Djégoumana. He assured me that his people would willingly do the donkey work and agreed that they would definitely need someone who understood the problem and the nature of springs to take charge. Apart from that, he was worried about the cost of materials that might be required. His people were subsistence farmers and forest gatherers, he pointed out. They seldom had, or needed, money. And, because of the water problem, they had very little spare produce to barter for materials.

My work was taking me northwards, to the fringes of the Sahara, and I would be away for six weeks. I explained this to Djégoumana and told him that on my return I would bring him someone who would stay in the village to work with his people and clean up the water supply. Materials would be no problem, because I had access to a small discretionary fund that would be more than enough to pay the small amount required.

He translated for the other villagers, who had accompanied our tour, and the news was greeted with great enthusiasm. When I told him that they would probably require large amounts of sand and gravel, he assured me that this was available locally and that he would set men to work straightaway on building up a stockpile. I suggested he wait until the new man arrived, as it might be necessary to grade the sand and it would be a shame to have to do the work twice over.

"That is why we need a boss!" he announced. "We do not know these things." Everyone nodded wisely.

I stayed a second night in the village and was fed on wild pig that one of the village hunters had speared in the forest that morning. The meat was succulent and tender and, washed down with more palm wine and accompanied by fascinating local folk tales, it contributed towards a most convivial evening.

Next morning, I drove back along the tortuous track and eventually turned north to resume my travels. Two weeks later, after several other visits, I reached Dargol in Niger.

I had come to visit a well-digging project run by volunteers from the American Peace Corps. Arnie Slomann, the volunteer who showed me round, had completed his time and was due to go home a week later. His replacement had arrived several days before and seemed to be settling in well. There was nothing now to hold Arnie back and he should have been raring to go. But he was not. Arnie was not a happy man. He came from Renoir, a small town in the Bushy Mountains of North Carolina, and spoke with an attractive sing-song drawl. He hated the flat desert of Niger, but had fallen in love with Africa and its peoples. He did not want to go home, but the Peace Corps would not extend his visa to permit him to stay.

Over the next few days, I inspected his work closely and watched how he got on with the local people. His command of the language was fluent. Learned on the job through living cheek by jowl with the local people, his ability to communicate was superb. His laconic manner and dry humour suited the desert and its people and Arnie was evidently well liked and respected. The work he had done was excellent, too.

"What are you going to do now, Arnie?" I asked as we left the final well site. "Go back to Renoir?"

"Reckon I'll look aroun' some first," he said.

"Won't your family be expecting you?"

"Nope. Tol' em not t'expec' me yet awhiles," he almost chanted.

"Would you be interested in another job like this in Africa?" I offered.

"Where?"

"Amèzodjikopé," I said cryptically.

"Whereinhellz'at?" he demanded, looking surprised.

"Down south a bit. Mountains and forest. It's an isolated village miles from anywhere, five or six hours on from where the road ends."

"Sounds good. Okay by me. So what they need done?" His decision made, he looked brighter already.

I explained in some detail and watched his enthusiasm grow. By the time I had finished, you would have thought he had just been given a million dollars. I offered to pick him up on my way back.

"Naw," he said. "Guess I'll kitch a ride on a truck, 'n then visit a bit on the way down."

He refused my offer of money to pay for his trip, but took some with which to buy materials and tools. He said he would have the essentials ready when I picked him up. We arranged to meet three weeks later in Atakpamé, after which I left him and continued my tour.

Three weeks later, we met as arranged and Arnie had a stack of tools and materials ready for loading into the Landrover. He had enjoyed the journey southwards and was in high spirits. He told me all about his adventures as we headed west to Kouniohou. We stayed there overnight and set out early the next morning on the slow, barely visible track to Amèzodjikopé. The vehicle was now heavily loaded and frequently hit the stops on the suspension. We did almost the whole trip in low ratio four-wheel drive, and still struggled in places.

Our arrival in the village was greeted with a welcome similar to that I which had received on my first visit. Djégoumana was delighted when I introduced Arnie and told him that this was the man I had promised to bring. He immediately gave instructions for a vacant hut to be cleaned out and prepared for Arnie. Palm wine and toasted corncobs were produced as before.

When Arnie told him that we had brought tools and materials, the headman asked what sort of store they would require.

"Jist a space," came the laconic reply.

"What about the cement?" I asked.

"Got me some plastic. I'll make a platform 'n wrap it," replied Arnie, with a grin. He had been in the desert for a couple of years and was used to making do with almost nothing.

I translated what he had said into French and the headman sent two young men off to cut poles from the forest. He was adamant that the store should have at least a rudimentary covering, as the equipment and materials were obviously important and valuable. He then launched into a lengthy harangue of his people that seemed to be instructions about building the store, before turning his beaming face back to us.

As soon as the palm wine had been drunk, we set to and started unloading all the materials. Many willing hands made this easy, with everyone wanting to join in, and the whole lot had soon been carried into the village clearing. By the time the last load was brought in, the men who had gone to cut poles were back and Arnie was already working with them on constructing a platform for the store. It was all done within an hour. A framework had been erected, ready to be thatched the next day to provide a roof. Everyone seemed pleased with their effort.

During the journey to the village, Arnie had confessed to me that his French was, at best, rudimentary and I had wondered how he would get on in explaining things to the villagers. As far as I knew, only Djégoumana spoke French and the language here was very different from that used by the people Arnie had been working with before. I asked how he would manage?

"Why, I only has to show 'em 'till'n I learn their words," he said, as if it was the simplest thing in the world. "Don't allus need words if'n you want som'n done, but I'll soon learn the lingo."

That afternoon's work had proved that his confidence was well placed and I had no further doubts about his ability to work effectively with these people. This backwoods boy was already making himself welcome and at home here.

While Arnie wandered off around the village to start making friends, I sat down with Djégoumana to explain what I had arranged. He was pleased, and his translation to the villagers gathered around us brought smiles, nods of agreement and excited comments from everyone.

That night I shared Arnie's hut. The villagers had provided us with fresh grass mats to sleep on. Thick and springy, these made a very comfortable bed. I was surprised to see that the only thing Arnie had with him was a small goatskin duffel bag, with a large bowie knife tied to the outside by a leather thong. This apparently contained all his worldly possessions and was, he insisted, all he needed.

In the morning, we made a tour of the fouled stream and nearby springs. Arnie and I discussed the problem and the work that would need to be done as we headed back to the village. During the tour he had produced a small notebook and a pencil. Using me as interpreter for his inadequate French, he asked Djégoumana the local words for things he would need to know or tell others about, carefully noting the replies in his little book. By the time we reached the village, he was satisfied that he had learned enough to get started. Work would begin that afternoon. Djégoumana and the others were delighted.

Declining another session of palm wine drinking on the grounds that it would make me unable to drive on the forest track, I took my leave. I would be travelling north again in about a month and promised that I would call again during that trip. In the meantime, Arnie was to send me a shopping list for any other equipment or supplies he required and I would bring the items with me. Arnie walked out to the vehicle and waved me off. Looking in the mirror as I drove away, I could see him deep in conversation with a couple of the villagers.

Arnie's list arrived in the mail three weeks later. I was surprised by how little he had asked for, and it took less than an hour to collect most of it. The only item on his list that I had difficulty in finding was the selection of seeds he had requested, some of them for flowers. These were eventually produced by a friend, who brought them back from Accra the day before I was due to leave. The next morning, I bought a few additional items that I thought Arnie might find useful, loaded the Landrover and set of on my third visit to Amèzodjikopé.

There were few people about when I reached the village, but it did not take long for a merry crowd of children to arrive. Their faces were all smiling and there were constant shrill cries of "Ambeke!" My inability to speak to people in the absence of Djégoumana proved to be no impediment on this occasion. One of the boys grasped my hand, crying "Arnie! Arnie!" as he led me towards the forest.

I followed willingly and twenty minutes later we arrived at one of the springs, where Arnie and about twenty men were hard at work. They had excavated a huge hole in the hillside from which water now flowed in a clear bright trickle. A large pile of rocks had been collected beside a heap of sand. From time to time women arrived with baskets on their heads and added to one or other of these piles. Some of the men were mixing cement, while three others were laying stones to build a thick rectangular wall.

The work was going well and Arnie was obviously pleased. Djégoumana arrived and expressed his satisfaction in glowing terms. This was apparently not the only work being done. Two more groups were hard at work on other springs nearby. Arnie left what he had been doing and accompanied Djégoumana and I to inspect these. Both had reached a similar stage of construction, and from each a clear stream of sweet water flowed.

Watching Arnie with the workmen, I was surprised by how well he was able to talk to them. After only a month he had a remarkable working knowledge of the language and was continually trying to pick up new words and having his efforts laughingly corrected by the villagers. The headman and his people were impressed, too, and everyone joined in to help him learn, even the children. As we walked back to the village, Djégoumana told me that Arnie had contributed in other ways than just the work on the water supplies.

I was aware that Arnie had brought a number of iron bars and plates with him because I had helped to unload them, but the anvil that he had somehow obtained had escaped my notice at the time. Within a few days, he had built a small forge outside his hut. He repaired the villagers' tools and made new ones as they were needed. He had also shown them a new method of burning wood to make charcoal that produced a cleaner, hotter burning fuel for both his forge and the village cooking fires.

When I asked him about all these little extras, Arnie just shrugged them off as nothing out of the ordinary.

"Heck! I only done what we allus duz back home. If'n we needs some'n, we makes it," he told me.

"What about the charcoal?" I asked.

"Now there's a s'prize!" he sang. "The carbon they make here's good burnin' fuel, but it crumbles and breaks up too easy. I wanted good hard pieces for the filters. So, I teach 'em how to burn f'r it. It was jus' lucky that it turned out to be a better fuel as well. But it'll sure make good filters."

There was no answer for that, so all I could do was admire his resourcefulness and hand over the few supplies he had requested.

My work then took me northwards once more, to the fringes of the Sahara, so it was some months before I visited Amèzodjikopé again. As before, Arnie had sent me another meagre shopping list for tools and a few materials. The only thing that puzzled me this time was his request for kiln cones. Reasoning that he never asked for anything unless it was important, and unable to find any locally, I had a box sent out from a pottery in England.

When I arrived this time, the work on the four springs nearest the village was complete. Each one now had a large stone-walled filter box that gave a steady stream of crystal water. Djégoumana and his people were delighted. Once again they had time to work in their fields, to hunt in the forest and to gather fruits, berries and wild honey. Nobody had been sick since my last visit. This time, before offering palm wine, Djégoumana gave me a gourd of clean sweet water with a gesture of reverence that told how richly this was valued.

The kiln cones were soon explained when I spoke to Arnie. He was not setting up as a potter, as I had suspected, but, together with the village potters, was experimenting to see if it would be possible to produce their own clay water pipes.

The nearest spring was still almost a kilometre from the village and it took the women the best part of an hour to walk there and return with a few gallons of water and each woman was making at least two trips a day to supply her household. Arnie had surveyed the ground and had decided that it would be possible to lay a pipeline and bring the water direct to the village. To do this, he required pipes and a tank. The tank was already under construction just outside the stockade and would soon be completed. The pipes he proposed to make out of fired clay.

The village potters had tried several times to produce short lengths of earthenware pipe, but had only succeeded up to a point. The main problem was that they were unable to fire them at consistently high enough temperatures to vitrify the clay, so that the results were both fragile and porous. Arnie had built a proper kiln and needed the cones to check the firing temperature. Once they could get that right every time he would use the steel sheets I had brought to make proper moulds for the pipes. Then they would go into production.

I asked him why he had not simply asked me to get some plastic pipe.

"It don't last, 'n' when it breaks you has to pay fer the mendin' even if'n you does it y'self. The people own the pipes we make here so they's keen to fix it if'n some'n goes wrong. We got plenty time to make the pipes, 'n' since they ain't never had one, they ain't impatient to be finished. What we c'n make here everyone understands. If'n they cain't understand some'n they don't trust it so they don't use it right," he explained in what, for Arnie, was a long speech.

He made it all sound so simple, but I remembered from my own attempts to make pots at school how easily things could go wrong. Even so, his commitment was infectious and it was easy to believe in Arnie's dream. I handed over the box of cones and he rushed off to summon the potters so that they could fire up the kiln.

Time flies when there is work to do. By the time I next visited the village, Arnie had been at Amèzodjikopé for nine months. As I pulled up outside the stockade, I hardly recognised the place. It looked like a completely different village.

The stockade was festooned with rampant creepers bearing a profusion of gaudy blooms and fruits. Inside, the scene was similarly transformed. The walls of many of the houses were now painted white. Most of them had small clumps of bright flowers growing beside them. Arnie's house was surrounded by zinnias and marigolds and the headman's house was almost overgrown with morning glory and moon flowers.

Djégoumana was amused by my reaction and proud of his village. The people liked the flowers and their lives were now easier than at any time he could remember. The fields had given a good crop because people had had time to tend them, and there had been no more sickness.

The tank by the village gate was now finished, with the stonework smartly pointed. The potters had been successful in making good vitreous pipes and the line from the nearest spring was complete and working. As luck would have it, I had arrived on the day that the new tank was first filled and none of the women had gone more than fifty paces beyond the stockade to fetch water that morning.

Djégoumana was lyrical in his praise, not only of Arnie's efforts, but also of the villagers, all of whom had embraced the new ideas with enthusiasm and had worked diligently at helping to implement them. The delight in his eyes and the richness of his voice gave me a warm glow when he thanked me for finding Arnie and bringing him to Amèzodjikopé.

Arnie was talking like a native when I came across him sitting with a group of men, discussing some new project. When I remarked on his fluency, he shrugged off my compliment in his usual laconic manner.

"They'm good teachers," he said.

"You've done a good job here. Where are you going to go now?" I asked.

"Oh, there's still plenty to do here," he replied.

"Don't you want to go home to Renoir?"

"Nope. This is ma home."

"What about your family, won't they be missing you?"

"Don't reckon. There's the old folks an' nine brothers an' four sisters to mind the farm. Don't need me. Reckon I'll jist stay here," he answered.

"What? Permanently?" I was surprised.

"Yup," he nodded. "Wan' a beer? I made a brew."

He went into his hut and returned with a glazed stoneware bottle. It was remarkably good beer and I forbore asking how he had managed to produce it. Arnie was so full of inventiveness that nothing he did could surprise me any more. His resourcefulness seemed to have no bounds.

I left him and went to talk with Djégoumana. Arnie had already mentioned his desire to stay to the headman and I asked what he thought of the idea.

"He is welcome. This has become his home now," he told me. "But I have one concern and wish to ask your advice. If he will stay here he should have a wife. Does he have one in his own country?"

"No. He has no wife," I said.

"Well, we have several girls ready for marriage. Any of them would make a good wife. What do you think, will he have one of them?"

"It's certainly something for him to think about," I said. "Have you asked him?"

At that moment Arnie arrived, so I put the idea to him.

"S'pose it'd make sense," he said with a shy grin. "Cain't say as I've thought about it, bein' so busy an' all."

"Well, would you want a wife and family if you're going to stay?" I asked him.

"Guess so."

"Anyone in mind? A girl at home you'd want to bring over, or someone else more local?"

"Nope. Ain't never considered it yet."

I explained this exchange to Djégoumana who roared with laughter. "That is no problem!" he said, "The maidens here all have eyes for you, Arnie! We caught an antelope in the forest this morning. We shall have a feast tonight to celebrate the new water tank. Later, when the maidens dance, you shall choose."

The whole village was in festive mood that night and the feasting was accompanied by energetic drumming, dancing and singing. Vast quantities of food were consumed and, along with the usual calabash of palm wine, Arnie produced many bottles of his new beer. It was a wonderful celebration that did justice to all the hard work that had been done; to the innovation and new skills that had been developed; and to Arnie's decision to make Amèzodjikopé his home. This last seemed to be universally popular.

Late in the evening, at a signal from the headman, the drums abruptly ceased their pulsing rhythms. Those who had been dancing sat down around the dancing ground. More wood was thrown on the two fires at each end of the open space to make them flare and burn more brightly. A single drummer started a quiet beat and the susurration of conversation died, leaving an air of breathless anticipation.

Another signal from Djégoumana brought twenty-two young women onto the dancing ground to stand in line, facing the headman and assembled elders. Apart from a bunch of leaves before and behind, suspended for modesty on a waistband of beads, the girls were naked. All in their late teens, they were beautiful girls in the full bloom of youth. Hair had been elaborately coifed with intricate plaits, beads and feathers. Bodies had been oiled until they glowed. Bracelets and anklets of cowrie shells rustled with every move and step.

A second drummer joined the first, then a third beat a counter point rhythm and the girls began to dance. At first they danced in line, stepping, bowing, turning. As the beat changed, the line began to sway then shift as the girls moved through an intricate sequence of steps, weaving in and out of the line.

The pattern developed with skips and jumps as other musicians joined the accompaniment. The whole scene was graceful and erotic, with breasts and buttocks thrust proudly out, arms moving sinuously, legs strutting and thrusting powerfully. And, from time to time, there would be subtle glances towards the village bachelors, whom the girls were trying to entice. The performance went on for almost half an hour, the patterns of movement and rhythm constantly changing. The lithe young bodies glistened in the glow of the flickering flames at each end of the dancing ground.

A change in rhythm from the drums brought the sequence to an end and the line untangled itself like a snake uncoiling, until the girls were back in the positions where they had begun. Then the dance was over and the audience, who had remained silent and still throughout, erupted into applause and cheering.

Djégoumana rose, taking Arnie by the hand and leading him out onto the ground in front of the line of smiling girls. He turned to face the elders as the village fell silent.

"This man needs a wife to make his home here," he announced in a rich tone. "These maidens are of an age to be married and each needs a husband. Shall he take one of these?"

"Choose! Choose! Choose!" chanted every voice in the village.

Djégoumana turned Arnie to face the line of girls.

"Choose!" he said and pushed Arnie gently towards them.

Arnie stumbled to a halt, looking extremely confused, and just stared at the line of beauties arranged before him.

"Go and look closely," Djégoumana urged, pushing him firmly towards the girls.

Arnie moved towards one end of the line as the solo drummer picked up a soft pulsing rhythm that was both erotic and compelling. As he moved slowly along the line, the girls smiled at him, each, in turn, posing provocatively. He reached the end of the line and then, scratching his head and looking even more bemused than ever, went back for a second inspection.

The girls began to giggle and wiggle their hips enticingly as he moved slowly down the line once more. At the end he scratched his head again and turned to the headman with a shy smile.

"They'm all so priddy. How kin I choose one?"

"But you have not examined them!" Djégoumana exclaimed, throwing his arms wide in dismay. "Look! Like this!" He moved to the first girl, reached out with both hands and grasped her breasts. The girl giggled and rolled her eyes. "Examine them properly and then choose!" The headman urged him again.

Arnie hesitated. The girl reached forward, grabbed his wrists and lifted his hands to her thrusting breasts. Arnie grinned and gave her a squeeze. The girl giggled again and wriggled with delight. With a smile Arnie moved on. After examining a couple of girls in this manner, he got into the spirit of the occasion and began to enjoy himself. He went up and down the line twice, his eyes flashing in the flickering firelight and his face wrapped in a huge smirk of absolute pleasure.

The girls were obviously enjoying themselves too, and looked disappointed when he did not return for a third tour. They made loud kissing noises and waggled their fingers at him.

"They'm all so beautiful. How kin I choose one?" Arnie repeated.

"Then choose two!" Djégoumana replied to great applause from the villagers and a rousing cheer from the girls.

Arnie went up and down the line again to the obvious delight of the girls. They leaned into his hands and ran their fingers through his hair and down his arms. When he came to the end of the line this time, Arnie went round the back and felt all the girls' buttocks. This was greeted with howls of laughter and hoots of delight from villagers and girls alike.

At last he came back and everyone fell silent.

"They'm all so beautiful," he said, spreading his hands. "The choice's too diffcult f'r a simple country boy."

Djégoumana's wife went forward and whispered in her husband's ear for several moments. He smiled, obviously accepting her suggestion, and turned to Arnie again.

"Then the girls shall choose. Will you accept their choice?"

"Why, sure," Arnie agreed, whereupon Djégoumana turned to the line of waiting maidens and told them to make the choice.

The girls skipped into a huddle and the women among the audience broke into song. The conference went on for several minutes before the group separated. Most of the girls moved back to the edge of the dancing ground, leaving two who turned to face Arnie and Djégoumana. The crowd again fell silent.

In unison, those who had moved back shouted: "We have chosen! These two are your wives – Aniani and Iusunu."

Once again, the villagers erupted into applause and cheering. The drummers beat out a vigorous tempo and the two girls began to dance, on their own, in the centre of the ground. Arnie looked somewhat surprised and then walked purposefully over to his hut. Several young men followed him inside and a bright curtain was drawn across the doorway.

As Djégoumana resumed his seat, two men came and squatted

next to him.

"You must name the bride price," their headman told them.

"He has done much work in my pottery and taught me new things that will benefit everyone. The price is paid by this," said one of the two. "I take him as my son."

"He has cleaned our water and brought it to the village. He makes new tools that we can all use. The price is paid by these things," the blacksmith said. "I also take him as my son."

"It is settled," said the headman, with a nod, and all three shook hands.

The two girls continued their dance in the centre of the ground, looking round occasionally at Arnie's hut, as if waiting for something. A few minutes later the curtain was drawn aside and Arnie emerged. The crowd cheered and started a new chant. The drummers changed their rhythm to one that was more complex, subtle and provocative as Arnie was led out onto the dancing ground by his friends.

They had cut off his shoulder length hair and left just fine stubble. His beard had also been trimmed short, making him look much younger. Dressed now in nothing but two bunches of shiny leaves and a beaded belt, his oiled skin glowing in the light from the two fires, Arnie was led forwards to dance with his new wives.

He managed to look proud, masterful and intensely happy all at the same time as he and the two brides circled, stamped and wove their way through the nuptial dance. The crowd around the dancing ground stood, stamped, shuffled and clapped the tempo in a slow moving circle around them.

The three of them danced for over half an hour before the drummers changed the beat and the parents of the two brides moved forward to join them on the dancing ground. At the next change, Djégoumana and the village elders also joined in and an intricate pattern of movement developed. After perhaps another half an hour, the beat changed yet again and everyone else leapt onto the dancing ground to join the action.

As dawn began to streak the eastern sky with red, the two brides' fathers took them towards Arnie's hut. The crowd parted to let them through, though the momentum of the dancing never faltered. At the entrance, the fathers stripped the leaves from their daughters and pushed them both inside. They then sat themselves down on either side of the doorway.

The two mothers brought Arnie to his hut. At the entrance they removed his leaves and both bent to inspect his equipment before pushing him inside with his brides. The two women then sat down with their husbands to await the outcome, while the rest of the village returned their attention to the dancing.

By mid morning, the crowd had thinned a little and Djégoumana was sitting with me, catching a few minutes rest and drinking strong black tea. The two fathers approached and sat with us.

"We have a good son," the potter said. "Our daughters are both women and wives now."

"Twice!" said the other with a wicked grin.

The celebrations continued for another two days. Never once did the drumming cease, and never once were there less than thirty people on the dancing ground. Food was brought in relays and people stopped briefly to eat before resuming. Bowls of food were taken to Arnie's hut and pushed inside, beyond the bright curtain that had been drawn across the doorway when the brides' parents had ended their vigil in the middle of the first morning. Neither Arnie nor his brides emerged from the hut until dawn on the second day.

It was the wives who emerged first, hastily tying gaily coloured lengths of cloth around their bodies as they were pursued by their shouting husband.

"Get out you lazy women!" Arnie was shouting, "There's work to do, water to fetch. Look at the mess in this house! Where's the food? Have you nothing better to do than lie on the mat all day? Get out and work before I decide you'm worthless and send you back to your fathers!" He finished the tirade off with a smart slap to each girl's backside that neither tried to avoid and both evidently enjoyed.

The girls ran off to do his bidding and Arnie went back into his hut, pulled on a pair of shorts and ambled over to sit with Djégoumana and me.

"I see your wives obey you well," the headman observed.

"Their fathers told me I should beat them, but they'm too priddy. 'Tis nough to shout," Arnie replied.

"Maybe that is better," smiled Djégoumana. "Now the whole village knows you are their master."

"As you are our master," Arnie replied.

The headman looked pleased. The protocols had been observed, the traditions upheld, and the future secured by binding Arnie to his community.

By the time I eventually I left Amèzodjikopé, I was exhausted. After fifteen kilometres, I stopped the Landrover, climbed into the back and slept solidly for six hours before resuming the arduous drive back to the outside world and work.

My next visit was about three months later. As I walked into the village Aniani and Iusunu rushed to greet me. Each hugged me warmly and gave me a fat kiss on the forehead, saying: "Thank you for bringing us our husband." I was enormously flattered by this unexpected gesture and by the warmth of the welcome I received from them. Arnie was his usual laconic self.

"How are you Arnie? I asked. "Got any new projects going?"

"Aw, fine," he said, "Busy plantin' a new field. Got wives to feed."

"They both look well and happy," I remarked.

"Aw, fine," he grinned. "Come back in six months 'n' we'll have 'nother party. They'm both expectin'."

The Missionary's Feet

The Reverend Bernard Cornwell had been a missionary in Africa for over twenty-seven years, the last seventeen of which had been spent as the incumbent at Ifiet Ikomo, a riverine mission in the forests of the Niger delta.

His years at the mission had been happy ones. He had built up a strong congregation, who regularly attended services and who also came to the mission for weddings and christenings. He was well received in all the surrounding villages and it would be fair to say that the people loved him.

His wife, unable to bear children of her own, fulfilled her maternal instincts by helping the women of the area with theirs. She talked little of religion, believing that this was rightly the province of an ordained man and therefore something into which a wife should not intrude. Instead, Mrs. Cornwell took a practical interest in the welfare of both the present and future generations. She started a primary school at which mothers were welcome to come and learn alongside their children. Even one or two fathers made tentative efforts to learn to read and write. Like her husband, Mrs. Cornwell was loved by the people.

While many others packed up and left during the Biafran war, the Cornwells stayed at their mission and continued their work as if nothing had changed. Indeed, apart from the need to set up a First Aid post and feeding programmes for refugees from the conflict, nothing much did change. Aircraft occasionally passed overhead and the sounds of gunfire or exploding bombs could sometimes be heard in the distance, but there was no fighting in the immediate vicinity. Quite a number of wounded people appeared from time to time, although no soldiers from either side ever arrived in Ifiet Ikomo.

When the war was over, life soon resumed its normal placid

pattern and the Cornwells were regular participants in many of their community's activities.

Bernard Cornwell's sudden death from a heart attack came as a shock to everyone. Many of his congregation assembled outside the simple thatched bungalow of the mission house in silent vigil. They stayed for two days, until a doctor was brought to certify the death.

The minister from a neighbouring mission, forty miles away, came to conduct the service. Bernard Cornwell was laid to rest in the mission cemetery alongside the fifty or so of his converts who had joined the celestial flock before him.

Having spent so much of her life at Ifiet Ikomo, Mrs. Cornwell considered it her home. All her friends were there, her work was there, and she had no desire to be anywhere else. The Missionary Society, which had sent the Cornwells out to Africa, took a different view and would not countenance her staying on alone. She felt betrayed and pleaded to be allowed to stay, but the Society was adamant.

With great sadness, she departed to a lonely existence in Durham, a city where she knew nobody and that she had not visited since her marriage, over thirty years before. In Ifiet Ikomo, the villagers showered her with gifts and held a great feast in thanksgiving for all her years of selfless work among them. The singing and dancing went on for two energetic days, but the taint of sadness at what amounted to a second bereavement within a month touched everyone.

On the day of Mrs. Cornwell's departure, her few possessions and the many bundles and baskets of gifts were loaded into the mission's old launch and tearful embraces were exchanged for the last time. All the village fishing canoes were crammed with people as they accompanied her on the first stage of her journey. Naturally, as with any event of sad significance in this part of the world, there was a great deal of wailing and weeping, with exhortations to return, and a constant chant from the village 'praise singer', extolling their departing friend's innumerable virtues.

Eventually the canoes turned back and, in subdued silence, the people returned to their village to nurse their grief. With no ordained minister to lead them, the members of the congregation felt lost. The minister who had conducted the funeral came from time to time to take services, but the people did not know him, and their numbers began to dwindle. Soon, the frequency of the minister's visits started to decrease – from once a month to once every six weeks, then once every ten weeks and, eventually, once every four months. With their faith undernourished, the people gradually slipped back into their former animist traditions and beliefs, and Christianity was relegated to history in all but a few staunch hearts.

One old man, half blind and rickety, stayed on at the silent mission as caretaker. There was little enough for him to do, his only duties being to stop the surrounding jungle from encroaching while also ensuring that any storm damage to the buildings was repaired. Otherwise, the place was deserted and unused. It remained this way for a long time.

The death of Bernard Cornwell had come at a most inconvenient time for the Missionary Society. They were short of trained staff, finance was still tight after the costly relief efforts made during various wars around the world, and a number of other missions had also experienced setbacks. As a result, it was almost two years before a new man was appointed to reopen the mission at Ifiet Ikomo.

Robert Sinclair was a reserved man with a strong faith and a quiet enthusiasm as yet untarnished by the frustrating realities of missionary life in the field. He had worked for the Society, in an administrative capacity at their headquarters, for six years after his ordination. This was his first appointment overseas.

His wife was city bred and of a shy, slightly timid disposition. She seemed an unlikely candidate for missionary work, but her solid faith and quiet, unwavering support for her husband were seen as admirable qualities by those who made such decisions. In addition, she was an experienced teacher who had worked among deprived inner city urchins and had achieved excellent results.

The couple were both in their early thirties, childless as yet, and largely naïve to the ways of the outside world. During the sea voyage along the West African coast, the colourful sights and sounds they experienced in each of the ports at which their ship called, all so exotically foreign to them, provided a constant series of surprises and wonders.

Having transferred from the ship to a launch for the last stage of their voyage through the winding channels of the delta and up river, the entire character of their long journey changed dramatically. One moment they would be marvelling at the untamed natural beauty of the forest only to be plunged, minutes later, into the depths of despair at the shocking scenes of destitution that greeted them in many of the villages along the riverbanks. The primitive simplicity of life in the delta was, at various times both savage and beautiful to them.

Although the conflict had been over for some years, the depredations of war were still visible. Disease, poverty and squalor were endemic, and all too obvious. The sight of maimed adults and pot bellied children with runny, fly-blown noses produced a surge of compassion in them both and they felt even more certain that they were doing the right thing coming to Africa.

Word had been sent ahead to Ifiet Ikomo that the Sinclairs would be coming to reopen the mission, but nobody had known in advance exactly when they were to arrive. However, their progress up river was slow and sedate in the old launch, so news of their coming soon spread along the riverbank communities and by the time they reached the mission jetty at Ifiet Ikomo, late on a Friday evening, several dozen of those who had kept the faith were assembled on the riverbank to welcome them.

As the launch rounded the final bend and came into view, the gathering burst into song and began to dance. Others, attracted by the noise, soon joined them and by the time the launch had made fast to the wooden jetty the crowd was several hundred strong. A man who had served as a sort of Church Warden under Reverend Cornwell came forward and greeted them without introducing himself by name.

In preparation for their new posting, the Sinclairs had taken language lessons, but this was their first real opportunity to practice their new skills. Any lack of fluency mattered little that first evening, for they were swept along on a tide of smiling, singing faces that bore them inexorably through the village and on towards the mission. They soon found that ready smiles were all that was required of them in return, since the noise was such that nobody could have understood them even if they had tried to speak.

At the door of the mission house, there was some confusion. The door was locked and nobody appeared to have the key. The old caretaker was now almost completely blind and in the first stages of senility. Helpful villagers rifled through his hut in search of the key, but found nothing. Others tried the mission windows, but these were tightly shuttered and bolted from the inside.

After twenty minutes or so of this confusion, the village elders arrived. They invited the Sinclairs to return to the village and eat with them. While they were doing this, the key would be found and someone would sweep out and prepare the house. Hungry and weary after their long journey, the Sinclairs gladly accepted this invitation, conscious of the need to make a good first impression and to avoid offending their new parishioners.

The elders led their guests to an open-sided, thatched building in the centre of the village, where low, carved wooden chairs were set out around a platform of beaten clay. The meal that was served consisted of a succession of traditional local dishes in clay pots, wooden bowls and tightly woven baskets. By the flickering light of crude oil lamps and storm lanterns, the colours were muted and the visual impact of the food was soft and slightly mysterious, but the smells were strange, new and exotic. The Sinclairs had never tasted anything but the plainest of European fare and the novelty of the food and the dramatic tropical environment made the meal both tantalisingly exciting and yet at the same time totally unnerving, given the uncertainty about what these forest people might have put in the pot.

When a meat stew was offered, Mrs. Sinclair turned pale at the sight of roughly cut pieces of monkey, pangolin and tree rat – some still wearing their fur – floating in an oily red soup. The sour smell of *fou-fou* turned her already fragile stomach and the most she could do was to nibble at a few small spoonfuls of boiled rice, explaining that the journey had been so long that she was too tired to eat. The villagers noticed her discomfort and graciously accepted her excuse.

Robert Sinclair was made of stronger stuff. Hiding his initial revulsion, he tucked in with apparent relish. Watching the villagers' technique, he dipped his fingers into the food. Although it was spiced with hot chillies, he found it surprisingly tasty and his enthusiasm soon became genuine. He ate heartily, to the evident approval of his hosts.

After the meal had been followed by several speeches of welcome, the villagers took pity on the exhausted couple and escorted them back to the mission house.

Someone had found the key and the door stood open. The main room and the bedroom had been swept clean. The Sinclairs' baggage had been brought up from the jetty and piled against the wall in the main room. Water had been carried up from the river to fill the tank, which stood on a low wooden tower behind the bathroom, and someone had also washed out the bath and basin.

Remembering Mrs. Cornwell's delight in the forest flowers, one thoughtful villager had collected several gaudy orchids and placed them in an old beer bottle. This floral welcome now stood in the middle of the big table, facing the front door. The dim light of an oil lamp highlighted the display and lifted Mrs. Sinclair's tired spirit.

Simon, the Church Warden, had overseen the cleaning operation. He explained that it had taken some time to find the key, so not everything was finished as he would wish. However, the women would return in the morning to clean up the rest of the house and help the Sinclairs settle in. He would also see that the simple church was cleaned and ready to use.

The village elders, meanwhile, announced that they would prepare a proper welcome for the next day, during which they would also take their new friends on a tour of the village and the surrounding area. Eventually, everyone said good night and the Sinclairs were left alone. They were so tired by this time that they simply hung up their new mosquito net, spread sheets on the bed and collapsed together into a long, exhausted sleep.

The day was already several hours old by the time the couple woke in the morning. They found a group of chattering women outside, armed with brushes, cloths and baskets of fruit. The door was no sooner opened than this merry band swept in like a tidal wave to continue the previous evening's work. While the women swept and cleaned, the Sinclairs sat down to breakfast on a mountain of exotic and unfamiliar fruit that their new parishioners had thoughtfully provided.

They had hardly finished eating before the village elders arrived to give them a formal welcome and lead them out on the promised tour. The proceedings began with introductions to a long line of people whose names they promptly forgot. Then they were taken to inspect the church and the school before being shown round the whole area.

The new missionary and his wife expected this to be just a brief tour of the village, but the villagers and their elders had other ideas. They were marched round every compound in the village, then out into the surrounding fields. Once this was completed, they were taken back to the jetty and piled into the mission launch. Up and down the river, they visited all the communities that formed the parish of Ifiet Ikomo and were plied with food and drink in every one of them.

The welcome everywhere was one of noisy enthusiasm, and they found themselves overloaded with new impressions and new faces. It was after dark when they finally returned to Ifiet Ikomo, having visited over twenty other settlements. They were once again exhausted and, having already been given so much food, far too full to eat. Promising to hold full Sunday services the next day, the Sinclairs again collapsed into sleep, their baggage still untouched.

More fruit was delivered the next morning, as they prepared themselves for church. Whilst Robert Sinclair busied himself composing a few notes for his first sermon, his wife unpacked his clerical gowns and then got dressed herself. The rest of the day was taken up with services, bible classes and introductions to more individual parishioners. So, it was not until Monday that the Sinclairs had a proper opportunity to explore their new home and settle in.

The house had all the necessary basic furniture and the book-shelves still contained many volumes left behind by Mrs. Cornwell. The kitchen had a large iron wood-burning stove and, surprisingly, a refrigerator. This ran on paraffin, and Mrs. Sinclair was surprised to find that someone had kindly lit the burner.

Curiosity made her open the door and look inside. With a scream of terror, she then instantly slammed it shut again and fled from the kitchen.

Her husband was on his knees in the living room, unpacking their belongings from a trunk when the commotion broke out. He jumped to his feet as his screaming wife rushed into the room and buried her face in his chest, sobbing hysterically. Wondering what could have provoked this outburst , he calmly folded his arms around her and held her until she regained control. When her sobbing eventually subsided, he asked quietly what on earth it was that had upset her so much.

"There's a foot in the fridge!" came the muffled cry.

"Of course there's food in the fridge, my love," he said gently. "That's where you always keep it."

"Not food!" she said, pulling away from him. "A foot! There's a foot in the fridge. A human foot!!" And with that, she fled, weeping, to the bedroom.

Blinking in surprise at this outburst, Robert Sinclair stood watching, slightly stunned, as his wife disappeared into the room and slammed the door. He could hear her sobbing once again and was torn between a desire to go and make further efforts to comfort her and an overwhelming curiosity to look inside the refrigerator.

Curiosity prevailed and he made his way into the kitchen. Slowly and with a distinct feeling of apprehension, he eased the door of the fridge open – and gasped in surprise at what was revealed. There was indeed a foot there. Or rather, two feet! Closer inspection confirmed that there was another black foot behind the one glimpsed by his wife, the second one still attached to its lower leg. He peered more closely and saw that both appeared to have been cleanly severed from their owners.

Thoughtfully, he closed the refrigerator door on the gruesome contents and turned to look around the kitchen. The wooden table had been scrubbed clean, as had the white enamel sink. The stove had been prepared, but not yet lit.

He took a match and lit the kindling, filled the kettle from the earthen water jar and placed it over the fire. As the flames took hold, he fed more sticks into the fire box to produce a good blaze and then waited for the water to boil. A cup of tea would help his wife to recover from the shock. Meanwhile, his thoughts turned back to the grim contents of the refrigerator.

Robert Sinclair had heard tales of cannibalism among these people, but the people at the Society's headquarters had assured him that this had died out many years before. However, there had been a civil war since then and a number of old habits may have re-emerged. But no, he reasoned. He was being fanciful. There must be some quite innocent and probably very mundane explanation. He would have to ask the old caretaker and Simon. They had had charge of the mission while it was unoccupied and would no doubt know exactly what this was all about. Then he remembered how the key had been mysteriously missing when they came to open the house and he began to have misgivings. However hard he tried to rationalise things, gruesome possibilities still lurked in the back of his mind.

How long could the feet have been there anyway, he wondered. He opened the refrigerator door again. With a cautious finger he touched the first foot. Although it looked fresh, it was very cold. He noticed that the fridge was turned down to its lowest setting. He leaned forward and sniffed. There was only a slight odour, so the feet could not have been there more than a few days.

The sound of the lid of the kettle rattling as the water started to boil interrupted his train of thought. He made the tea and took it through to his wife with a tin of milk. Mrs Sinclair had calmed down a bit, but was still very upset.

"Did you . . ?" she began, hesitantly.

"Yes, I've had a look," he answered hurriedly, before she could complete the question, adding: "Don't touch anything. I am going to send for the police."

"But you must get rid of it, Robert!" his wife cried in alarm.

"And the fridge, too. I could never put food in it when there's been a human foot in there!"

"Feet," corrected Robert bluntly. "There's another one, with part of the leg attached. On the shelf, behind the one you saw."

His wife's eyes rolled up and she collapsed in a dead faint, spilling her tea over the bed. He quickly made her comfortable and waited until she had come round again, looking down at her with compassion and great love, then went to find Simon.

The Church Warden immediately became very uncomfortable when the missionary started questioning him.

"Who has been using the mission house?" asked Mr Sinclair.

"No wan, sah."

"Then who lit the refrigerator, and when?"

The Church Warden shrugged his ignorance like a small boy caught scrumping apples in the vicar's orchard.

"Why was the key not here when we arrived?" Sinclair continued. "Who had it?"

"I don' know. He gone away," Simon replied, evasively.

"Then where did you find it?"

"I ask him ebry wan where for him key do go. Den him come back," Simon muttered, shuffling his feet.

Sinclair decided to change tack.

"Whose feet are those in my refrigerator, then?"

"No wan, sah! No wan do go put him foot for fridge. Da's no clean!" He looked horrified at the suggestion.

"Then come and have a look," said Robert Sinclair, taking the reluctant man by the arm and marching him off towards the kitchen.

When the door was opened, Simon turned very pale and looked ill. Again, he denied all knowledge as to how the feet might have got there and hurried off with obvious relief when the missionary told him to go and bring the police.

It was two days before the local policeman turned up, two days during which Mrs. Sinclair stubbornly refused to go near the kitchen. As a result, they had to live off tea, boiled eggs and fruit, which was about the limit of Robert Sinclair's culinary ability.

The officer who eventually presented himself was a dapper little man with a round face and a neatly trimmed moustache. His blue uniform was immaculate and his shoes gleamed like mirrors. Although they had never met before, the man's face seemed oddly familiar to the missionary. It held that quality of authority and knowledge exhibited by experienced and worldly policemen the world over.

"I am Inspector Olosegun Okofumbwe," he announced, giving the missionary a smart salute. "How can I serve you, sah?"

"I have something to show you," Sinclair replied, and led him into the kitchen. He opened the small white door and pointed. "There."

The Inspector bent down and looked, then straightened.

"Oh yairs!" he said with a smile, "I know of dis one."

"But there are two."

"Ob corse! Ebry man hab two foots."

"Yes, but what are they doing in my refrigerator? Who put them there? And why?"

"Oh! I am put him foots deyah. Las' week," the Inspector told him. "Dis one crocodile he steal him one man for chop him. He don' eat him dis one foots and leavin' him for riva bank."

"But why are they here?"

"Dees one foots be hevidence. I hab to keep him fresh so I can making investigate for what happen dis time."

"But you said that you know what happened. The crocodile ate him. Surely you should dispose of them? Bury them or something? You cannot expect to leave them here."

"My job to investigate, sah," the Inspector said, his smile still firmly in place. "Police job is for make it very good investigation. I hab investigate ebryting an fin' dis one man be chop by crocodile. Dis my job is finish dis time. Now is youah job. Rebrend job to make burying. So, I am leave him dis one foots for you. Dis one now youah foots, so you can make it burying for hims."

Someone else came into the kitchen and Sinclair turned to find an embarrassed-looking Simon standing there, accompanied by a villager.

"What is it, Simon?" The missionary asked.

"Dis man is carpenta, sah," he replied. "I tell him make it coffin for you foots."

The other man came forward, holding out a neat wooden box.

"Very well, Simon. Put the feet in the box," he said and stepped back, turning away as Simon, still looking very uncomfortable, moved hesitantly towards the fridge.

Noticing his reluctance, the Inspector stepped forward smartly, brushed him aside and lifted the feet from the refridgerator, putting them in the box and then rather hastily replacing the lid.

That afternoon, in the presence of only the Inspector, the Church Warden, and the coffin maker, the missionary conducted his first funeral service at Ifiet Ikomo and buried the feet. When the tiny grave had been filled, Robert Sinclair solemnly shook hands with each man, thanked them for attending the ceremony and made his way slowly back to the mission house.

He went into the kitchen, turned off the refrigerator and removed its oil tank. He then carried it down to the river bank and rolled it into the water, watching as it sank out of sight into the murky depths. He paused for a moment on the river bank, deep in thought, before returning to the house. Back inside, he went to the kitchen, filled the kettle and put it on the fire.

He was somewhat distracted as he waited for the water to boil. The reason for his unease was an image that would remain engraved on his mind for evermore; that of the Inspector lifting the feet from the fridge and placing them in the little wooden coffin. It was in the moment before the lid was rather hurriedly replaced to cover up the gruesome contents that the missionary had realised something that he had not noticed before.

They were both left feet.

San Prison Blues

The wet season was proving to be the wrong time to try and make it to Timbuktu. This was my third attempt, and the road was again impassable. As fast as it was repaired – and, this being Mali, that usually took several months – another heavy tropical downpour would remove great sections of the road, often washing away stretches several kilometres long. At any other time I would simply have flown there, but my plane was grounded for a major overhaul and I was earthbound and reliant on an old Dodge Power Wagon that was on loan from one of the United Nations agencies.

I had managed to get as far as Goundam before I heard that the road had been washed away just beyond the town and reluctantly accepted that I would have to turn back. I spent a day in Goundam, looking around the market and talking to local people and, having found out a bit about the area, I decided to go back round the northern side of the Kabara lakes.

These are a curious geographical feature, with six tear drop shaped lakes, all approximately the same size, lying in a row at fifteen-kilometre intervals. They all drain into the north bank of the River Niger where it flows north-east through a series of shallow winding channels, and provide a haven for all sorts of birds and wildlife. They are also infested with crocodiles. To the south is a large area of swamp, on the eastern side of which is the ancient city of Mopti, where I had already been working for a spell some months previously.

After passing the sixth of the Kabara lakes, I turned south, hoping to pick up the road that I had been told led through the edge of the swamp and ended up in San. This would suit me well, as I needed to head east, back into Upper Volta, and the road from San would bring me to the frontier at Lekou.

Travelling along the north side of the River Niger, looking for a place to cross, I found and followed a track and, by a stroke of good fortune, very soon arrived at a village with a ferry capable of taking me and my vehicle across. I had to wait, of course, because as always on these occasions, the ferry was just approaching the far bank when I arrived and there was nobody on the other side waiting to come over. The ferryman would stay there until something turned up, so that he would not have to make a crossing without being paid for it.

Feeling hungry, I went in search of food, following the smell of cooking until I found a well patronised eatery a little further along the water front. Here, fortune smiled on me again when a man of about my own age approached me as I was eating and asked where I would be going once I had crossed the river. His name was Adoun and he was looking for a lift to San, where he was to rejoin his brother and his brother's family.

I liked him immediately and invited him to eat with me. Over the meal, we struck up a friendship. He and his brother were both fishermen and Adoun had been up to the Niger to do a little trading and to see if he could buy some new nets. He was friendly and open, with a constant smile on his face and a bright twinkle in his eye. I decided he would be excellent company on the journey south and as he assured me that he had been along that road a dozen or more times before, I felt confident that there was a reasonable chance we would not get too badly lost.

Eventually, a truck pulled up on the other bank and the ferry brought it across. With remarkably little delay, we were loaded aboard and transported safely across and, a few minutes later, had set off on the road south. It was a tortuous route, with numerous diversions, all of which Adoun had warned me about. For most of the way the road was bordered by very soggy swampland, with more than a few crocodiles, most of them about five feet long, basking on the mudbanks, soaking up the heat of the sun. We also saw a small flock of rather scrawny flamingos. This rather surprised me as I hadn't been aware that they came to this part of the world. Adoun told me that there actually used to be many more, but that they had caught some disease, as a result of which their numbers had greatly diminished over the last ten years. Disappointingly, they weren't very pink either.

Largely because of the diversions, we made slow progress, the whole journey taking us more than nineteen hours. We stopped a couple of times along the way, to eat and to stretch our legs after sitting for so long cramped up in the stuffy cab, and finally arrived in the wee small hours, tired but happy to have got there at last.

Adoun invited me to stay with him and his brother. There was no proper hotel and the only other accommodation was likely to be pretty squalid. He was most insistent, anxious to show his gratitude for the lift, so I gladly accepted.

It turned out that Midai really was his brother. I had wondered if this would actually be the rather tenuous sort of relationship that was common to the African extended family. However, Midai proudly showed me a photograph of the whole family, including another brother, two sisters and a whole flock of children, with the old mother and father seated in the centre.

The whole family made me very welcome and persuaded me to stay for a few days. The two brothers were keen to take me fishing in their pirogue to try out the new nets that Adoun had brought back with him. It looked very easy when they cast these nets, flinging them out in an arc so that they spread open like a flat disc before landing in the water, dragged down by the weighted edges. My own efforts were less successful, but provided endless amusement for my new friends, and for their family when we returned in the evening and they told the stories. It was precarious, standing up in the narrow dugout, and, in trying to cast the net, I nearly overturned the unstable craft several times. In the end, I resorted to a line of hooks and was rewarded with three large catfish. Adoun and Midai continued casting their nets and brought in over fifty assorted fish, all of a reasonable size.

When we returned to the house, Midai's wife produced a large bowl of *dolo*, the local millet beer. The one bowl was all we were getting, she informed us, as the rest was not really ready and, anyway, she wanted to keep it for the festival that was about to take place. I, of course, was curious and wanted to know what the festival was about and they immediately set about persuading me to stay another couple of days so that I could share it with them. I had time to spare so it didn't take too much arm-twisting to get me to extend my visit and I had a marvellous time, drinking liberal quantities of *dolo* and other local concoctions – although I never did find out quite what the celebrations were in aid of.

Looking back on it, if I had not allowed myself to be talked into staying the extra few days I would never have ended up in gaol. But I have no regrets. It was an interesting experience and it all worked out right in the end.

It all started the morning after the festivities were concluded.

While I and my new friends, along with most of the rest of the local population, were sleeping off the effects of a fantastic party, the local Chef Administratif – a sort of Governor, really – found out that I was in town and immediately took offence over the fact that I had not asked to stay with him and had not even been to offer formal greetings. That I had chosen to stay with a family of humble fishermen only made matters worse. He was upset.

In fact, he was so upset that he had the three of us arrested just before dawn and thrown into the local gaol.

Gaol here wasn't simply a matter of being locked up. It involved leg irons, manacles and an iron collar, all linked together with a heavy chain. The whole set weighed about thirty pounds and the end of the chain was padlocked to an iron ring on the prison wall. This was positioned so that the chain was just too short to enable one either to stand up straight or to lie down; so we ended up, like a hundred or so other hapless souls, having to crouch, or sitting with our hands raised and arms propped on our knees to support the weight of the manacles.

It was extremely uncomfortable, looked totally ridiculous and, to my mind at least, seemed extremely comical. I could not resist laughing as the ironmongery was put on and received a few good whacks from the warder's stick for my disrespectful behaviour. This made me laugh all the more, even though Midai and Adoun looked very depressed and hissed at me to stop.

As the warders walked away, I was thinking that this was just some silly joke and that we would be let out after an hour or so. Wrong! We were kept like this for four days and by the second day I could no longer see the funny side of it and had stopped laughing, although other prisoners maintained a constant round of cheering, singing and chain rattling.

Those irons were both heavy and uncomfortable. After only a few hours, the slightest movement brought excruciating pain and the skin was worn off so that my flesh oozed blood and attracted a cloud of unwelcome flies. Every effort to brush them off just made the pain worse and produced fresh blood to attract even more flies. I tried blowing them away, but this proved to be totally ineffective. I became increasingly concerned, imagining the flies bringing all sorts of infections and my hands and feet becoming gangrenous.

They don't feed prisoners in this part of the world, and unless a man has a family or friends to bring him food and water he has to go without. I suspect more than a few unfortunates have actually starved in such prisons. We were fortunate as Midai's wife and children came trooping in through the gate twice a day with baskets of food and large gourds of water. Midai looked slightly disappointed at the water and that evening his wife brought *dolo* and a bottle of *malafu*, the local palm wine. This was strong and made me slightly dizzy at first. Later, I realised that the ironmongery did not seem to hurt as much and did not feel as heavy. I decided it must be the effect of Amilada's alcoholic beverages.

On the fourth day, the Governor decided to inspect my vehicle, probably with the intention of seeing what he could find to confiscate. I have no idea what he found there that attracted his interest, but whatever it was it produced a marked change in attitude on his part and he came hot foot to the gaol and ordered my release, complete with apologies by the bucketful.

The warders hurried to remove my chains and even brought a bowl with some water and disinfectant so that I could wash the sores on my wrists and ankles. When it became apparent that only I was being released and that Adoun and Midai were to stay in prison, I protested strongly, but the Governor was adamant. So was I, however, and after a long argument that got absolutely nowhere, I sat down and snapped my irons back on, muttering about seeing the Minister of the Interior about this nonsense once I returned to Bamako, adding the warning that if I didn't turn up there soon someone would certainly come looking for me.

My performance produced much laughter and cheering from the other prisoners and the Governor, who was a short, fat, pale-skinned little man, danced with rage and grew more and more flushed. Eventually, the senior warder had a quiet word with him and he agreed that all three of us would be released. The warder advanced on me with his key, but I turned away and insisted that Adoun and Midai were released first. This produced more laughter and caused the Governor to become even more agitated.

Once my manacles were removed, his attitude changed and he became solicitous, trying to cover his embarrassment and regain the brownie points he had lost. I suspect he wanted to cover all his bets, just in case I really did have any influence with the Minister of the Interior. So desperate was he now to make amends that he even invited me to join him for lunch.

I nodded and told him that Adoun, Midai and I would be delighted to be his guests for lunch and watched with amusement as he bristled at the idea of having to entertain all three of us, struggling to control his already frayed temper. It was with the greatest reluctance – and only after I had stooped and made as if to pick up and replace the manacles that had just been removed – that he agreed.

It occurred to me at this point that I had better not overdo the pressure. At some time in the future it might prove useful to have this odious little official as a friend rather than an enemy. So I suggested that rather than going to the trouble of organising lunch for us at his residence, he should be my guest at the local restaurant.

The speed with which he accepted revealed him for the sort of man he undoubtedly was, but he still looked uncomfortable when I insisted that my two friends must come too. After all, they had endured four days in chains beside me and I had enjoyed their hospitality before that.

The restaurant proprietor never batted an eyelid and gave us the best table. I had to chuckle when Midai revealed that he usually came to the back door to sell his catch to the restaurant. Nevertheless, the man treated us all as honoured guests and served up an excellent meal of four courses. He even managed to produce a bottle of drinkable, though unremarkable, red wine. In an outpost such as this, that was something of an achievement, I felt, and I complimented him on it.

Lunch lasted until dark, so I agreed to stay another night in Midai's house and to visit the Governor officially, in his office, in the morning. I made a bit of a show of seeing him off at the door and he left as puffed up as a pouter pigeon. As he disappeared round the corner, I went back into the restaurant where the proprietor was sitting at the table with my two friends. His name, he said, was Ali Moudounassi-bis. I never found out why he was 'bis', but assumed he had a brother of that name who had predeceased his own birth. He had much enjoyed our visit, he told me.

He then called over one of his assistants and a case of cold beer was produced. He opened the bottles and handed them round, saying that it had been good to see the pompous Governor having to sit and eat with 'ordinary' people. He wanted to know all about our experiences in gaol and asked: "How was it in chains?"

All three of us erupted into laughter. Apparently it was known about all over town and dozens of people had gathered outside the walls to hear the singing and the laughter and the chain rattling that had gone on almost non-stop for the best part of four days. This would be the subject of discussion for a long time and was, Ali assured us, the stuff of which folk legends are born.

My friends and I staggered out of the restaurant at midnight, awash with beer and more excellent food, only to find another party in full swing back at Midai's house. Bowls of *dolo* and bottles of *malafu* circulated and we talked and sang and danced until sun-up. Adoun and Midai retold the saga countless times with great enthusiasm and, surprisingly, with very few embellishments. Not that the sorry tale needed any exaggeration; it had been such a farce.

I duly went to see the Governor again in the morning and once more endured his profuse and empty apologies for all the inconvenience and misunderstanding. I assured him that it was nothing important, that it would soon be forgotten and that I would make appropriate complimentary noises back in the capital. He looked more than relieved.

Before leaving, I asked his permission to take some food to the gaol – just some fruit and a few corncobs, that sort of thing. He agreed at once and sent a minion to warn the warder that I would be coming and to tell him to let me in. I left him and went to the market to buy the provisions.

One sack of toasted corn cobs, one sack of mangoes, one sack of ripe oranges, four cartons of cigarettes, a carton of matches and ten crates of bottled beer went into the back of my truck. As I approached the prison the broad gates were flung wide and I drove straight in. When the inmates realised what was happening they burst into song once more and rattled their chains with vigour. Laughter broke out when I asked the warders to distribute the food.

They bridled at first, but once I had made it plain that there was enough for them, too, they set about the task with enthusiasm and even took the chains off some of the prisoners so that they could help, joining in the laughter themselves.

Shaking hands all round took a long time, but eventually I left, with the sound of cheering, singing and laughter ringing in my ears. I could still hear it a mile away on the main road out of town, even above the noisy engine of the Dodge.

I stopped on the ridge for a few minutes, to take a final look back at San.

It is ironic, I thought as I turned onto the main road, that none of this would have happened and I would never have met all those lovely people had my plane not been grounded for a major overhaul.

Karma!

A Short Walk in Ituri

One of my lifelong ambitions had always been to visit the Ruwenzori Mountains. Their other name – The Mountains of the Moon – had appealed to me since childhood. So when the opportunity arose to accompany a group of Canadians to the area, the offer was too good to refuse. It was also too good to last.

In the late afternoon of the third day, just as we reached the tree line, Pierre Laporte suffered a heart attack and crumpled to the ground. His wife, Mirabelle, immediately scaled the heights of hysteria, demanding all sorts of assistance, rescue operations and instant emergency services that were totally unavailable in such a remote location.

The only option was to carry Pierre down the mountain and try to reach the vehicles that had been left behind in the foothills several days previously. Mirabelle demanded that we start down at once, but our three guides pointed out that this was not advisable as it would be dark in half an hour. The best idea would be to make camp, give everyone a hot meal, and let Pierre rest. To set out straightaway would not be sensible since we were all too tired to make the descent in safety, especially in the dark.

Our guides were experienced men, but Mirabelle was adamant and gave us a night of hell with a performance that made Shakespearean tragedy seem like light comedy by comparison. By dawn, she had so upset one of our Ugandan guides, Umoko, that he refused to continue with the party, declaring that he would rather forego his pay than remain in that woman's company any longer. He said he would carry on over the mountains and visit his brother, who lived on the western slopes.

I immediately asked Umoko if I could go with him. As I explained, I might never have another opportunity to see Ruwenzori and my presence was no longer required by the Canadians.

There was no need for me to return with them.

Umoko seemed dubious at first. "I may not come back for some weeks," he warned. "And I don't come back this way."

"That's OK. I can go down from the western side," I told him.

"To where?" he asked. "There is only thick jungle all the way to the Congo River on that side. No proper roads. Where do you go afterwards?"

"I have been working in Zaïre," I replied. "I have to go back there. Maybe I will go that way."

"It is not possible," Umoko declared in amazement. "There is the great forest, where even the animals cannot move freely. It is inhabited by bad men round the fringes and little black devils in its centre. Many bad things happen in that place. You should not go there."

I assured him that anything was preferable to continuing in the company of Mirabelle. On hearing this, he smiled his acceptance of my company and went to collect his gear.

"What's all this about little black devils?" I enquired as we picked up our packs and began climbing, leaving the Canadians to go back the way they had come, escorted by the other two guides.

"Pygmies," Umoko replied. "They do wicked things and worship strange spirits, and it is said they eat strangers. That is why nobody goes to that place," he added, with an air of finality.

Pygmies! A doorway had suddenly opened to another of my life-long dreams. I might now be able to visit Ruwenzori and the Ituri forest in the same trip.

I looked back. The Canadians had disappeared from view and I realised that we had moved over the shoulder of the mountain. Umoko and I were now on our own, heading up towards the snow line.

Below us the sparse trees, draped in hanging curtains of lichens and moss, had given way to open slopes dotted with the tall flower spikes of giant lobelia and the grotesque forms of unusual succulents and other species peculiar to these mountains. Where it was not covered with short tough grass or swards of delicate alpine flowers, the ground was strewn with large boulders. I could not understand how they had come to be there, but Umoko explained that they had been thrown out by a volcano to the south of our position, showering down on the landscape for many miles around.

In the dusk, he pointed to an orange glow on the southern horizon. "That is the mountain that never sleeps. Sometimes it spits rocks," he said. "Tomorrow night we will be higher. You can see him better then."

Umoko and I spent a whole week together exploring the Mountains of the Moon before following the western slopes downward towards more temperate levels. Only then did I realise how cold it had been up there. All my joints ached and my hands and feet tingled quite painfully from the returning circulation.

Four days after we started down from the higher levels, Umoko left me and went off in search of his brother. He pointed out the route ahead, but did not wish to accompany me any further. He was unwilling to enter Zaïre and had an intense dislike of the forest. He was a mountain man, he said. I think he was also a little afraid, judging by some of the tales he had been telling me about Ituri and its inhabitants.

Up in the high mountains it had been too cold to write much in my notebook. My fingers were so numb that I could not hold the pencil and I also kept getting cramp in my hand, so I had to content myself with seeing and trying to remember. I had only brought a small supply of film and had taken few photographs. Now, in the more temperate climate, I could again record my travels. My wristwatch, fortunately, showed the date.

3rd February. Umoko left me two days ago. The foothills on this side of the Ruwenzori are a mad lunar landscape of jumbled, broken rock with little growing on the open hillsides and dense, tangled vegetation in the many steep ravines. There are large areas of unstable scree, which take me hours to circumnavigate, and I have fallen heavily several times. Progress downwards is very slow and I estimate it will take at least another day to reach the Semliki River and the border with Zaïre.

As the ground flattens out, the vegetation changes and I find my feet ensnared in tangles of thorny vines that lurk beneath the waist high, glossy-leafed *ingwane* bushes.

5th February. I came to an area of dense forest two hours before reaching the river. There are few really big trees, but the ground cover is dense to a height of about five metres and the few game trails I have come across are overgrown and appear little used. The river is very low, with a large outcrop of rock on the far bank where I stopped to sharpen my machete. After washing in a pool below the rock, I decided to stay in this spot for the remainder of the day and rest.

I found some wonderful pink bananas growing a few metres back from the river. They are sweet and juicy, only a finger long, with creamy flesh and the most beautiful smell.

Throughout the afternoon, I lazed on the rock and absorbed the sunlight in the steamy heat. There were surprisingly few flies until sunset, when they arrived in their millions. In the gathering gloom, it took almost an hour of searching to find the right kind of leaves and prepare a pungent salve to keep the bugs at bay. Eventually, I managed to get a good smoky fire going and roasted a wild yam for my supper.

7th February. Late morning finds me sitting on a log beside a road. This is the first sign of human habitation that I have seen since Umoko and I parted company five days ago. Navigation has been somewhat erratic for the last few days and I'm not really sure where I am, but suspect that this must be the road between Beni and Irumu. I think I am somewhere about half way between these two villages. Logic tells me that I should visit one or the other to obtain supplies, but this will take at least two days and I want to get into the Ituri forest. This is just the fringe.

It is decision time. Two weeks of my leave have already gone and I have to be across the Congo River in twenty more days at the most in order to get back to work on time. Do I really need supplies? The forest people live off the jungle, so why can't I? Do I know enough to live off what it provides, without either poisoning myself or falling prey to some toxic plant or insect? Probably not, but there is only one way to find out!

On a clear patch beside the road, I have laid out all my kit to take stock of my resources:

- 1 rucksack (getting tatty),

- 1 pair of boots (starting to split), and a pair of sandals,
- 2 shirts (in need of washing),
- 1 pair of trousers (dirty but otherwise OK),
- 2 pairs of pants and a pair of shorts,
- 1 good pair of socks,
- 1 pair of holes pretending to be socks!
- a metal cooking pot and a plastic bag with a tin of matches
    (54 matches left)
- a knife and a machete
- canvas jacket
- Passport, money (Z74.40 remaining. I gave the last of my
    Ugandan money to Umoko when we parted).
- a small tin of seeds from Ruwenzori,
- a camera, 2 exposed films, 1 new film + one in the camera
    with 8 frames left,
- 2 notebooks (this and a full one)
- one and a half pencils and a dead biro,
- a prismatic compass and a torn, muddy, small scale map,
- and finally, me!

If I go for more supplies, it will be extra weight to carry. If I try to live off the forest I will certainly not go hungry, but could end up poisoning myself. Oh well, maybe someone will find my remains and guess what happened.

So, that's it then. To hell with going for supplies – I'm going into the forest. It may be the only chance I get to see Ituri and, possibly, the Pygmies.

8th February. Having made my decision, I had just finished packing my rucksack when I heard a vehicle coming and dived into the undergrowth to hide like a naughty child. I found myself resenting the presence of civilisation and wanting to avoid any renewed contact.

As I proceed deeper into the forest it has been hard going today, with bigger trees and dense growth on the forest floor and many small streams. The country is undulating, with low hills and shallow valleys. Now that I have entered the forest, the canopy has thickened overhead and such sunlight as reaches the forest floor is diffused and patchy. The light is quite subdued for much of the time, even at midday.

Near one small stream I came across a band of about twenty small grey monkeys, playing in the bushes and scampering up and down the surrounding trees. They seemed indifferent to my presence and, after watching them for twenty minutes, I moved on quietly and left them to their games. The forest is never quiet and I can hear all sorts of birds and other wildlife calling in the trees. Sadly, they are seldom visible as they flutter or scamper about their leafy domain. The cacophony diminishes slightly around noon, when all but the most hardy rest through the heat of the day, resuming just before dusk when new species join the chorus.

Moving through a particularly dense patch of undergrowth, I brushed against a plant with sharp edged leaves and made a deep gash in my right forearm. Blood flowed freely and within seconds clouds of voracious flies appeared, as if by magic. After washing the wound in a clear, bubbling stream, I laid a large green leaf over the cut, slapped on a generous coating of clay from the river bank and bound on a layer of soft bark, peeled from a nearby tree, as a bandage. In the absence of proper dressings, it seems to have worked well and I will just have to hope that there were no hostile microbes in the clay I used for the poultice, otherwise the arm could get very badly infected. There are no hospitals here, so I will just have to keep my fingers crossed.

During the late afternoon I came across a tree that makes relatively easy climbing, so I have installed myself thirty feet off the ground to sleep tonight. The ground here is soggy and it would be an uncomfortable place to bed down. The tree has large, thick leaves which, with a little redistribution, should keep me reasonably dry if it rains during the night.

12th February. I have stopped trying to write every day as it is not always practical. Sometimes it is too wet, sometimes too dark because of the dense canopy, and sometimes I just cannot find a suitable place to sit and scribble when I feel like doing so.

Today I crossed a bigger river. From my map I think this may be the Ituri River, which means I have now reached the edge of my objective. I have not encountered another soul since leaving Umoko, although I have smelled smoke on two occasions, so there may have been people not far away. The problem is, I don't know how far smoke smells may travel in the forest or how long they linger. The reference points I am most used to are of little use here and I have to learn a completely new set of indicators.

Most of the trees here are new to me and I only recognise about six species. There must be at least thirty more that I have never seen before. It is quite possible that some of them have never yet been identified and classified by botanists. This is a daunting thought in this modern age. How much more so must it have been to the early explorers of this continent?

I have been sampling fruits and nuts as I travel. Some are delicious, but one or two were bitter as sin and soon got spat out. So far, I have not experienced any ill effects, but the risk exists. I wish I knew more tropical botany!

Yesterday I found a clump of wild yams. These I do recognise, as they are similar to the *g'ubani* we had in West African forests. After digging around for a while with my machete, I took five medium-sized tubers and left at least three large ones in the ground. I have not yet been really hungry in the forest; in fact I am really quite well fed, such is the abundance of fruit and roots. However, I would enjoy some meat. My mind has turned to making snares and trying to catch something. I have also been trying out various vines and the fibrous bark from different plants in an effort to make a viable bowstring, but so far without much success. Raffia palms are either not common in this area or I have failed to see them; they would be the most useful for both bowstrings and snares.

In a moment of reflection, I realised that I am really enjoying this trip, even though I am progressing very slowly. I have probably covered no more than five or six miles today, still heading roughly north west.

13th February. Success at last. I now have a workable bow and four reasonably straight arrows with toasted hardwood tips. The only drawback is that since making them I have not seen any game to shoot at, so it all remains theoretical.

Early in the afternoon, I heard a couple of elephants. They were trumpeting and crashing about some way off to the south-west of me. I have no idea exactly how far away they were, but given the density of the jungle the distance cannot have been too great as the sound was quite clear. The difficulty is that I have no idea how far different sounds carry here. I scouted around for a while in the hope of seeing the elephants, but found neither tracks nor broken branches to show where they had been.

Game trails are more frequent in this part of the forest, and most appear better used than those I came across further east. I found a wild bees' nest today and tried to get some honey out with a stick. I got stung a dozen times for my insolence and ended up sucking the end of my stick for the very little honey that covered it. Perhaps I should have asked the bees' permission first.

There is so much to learn, but it's great fun!

Baked yam again for supper, with fresh fruit to follow.

14th February. I had been aware of the smell of smoke for a couple of hours as I walked this morning and eventually I heard noises of a distinctly human origin. Suddenly, the canopy overhead opened out and I found myself in a clearing with four crude buildings around its edge. One had had a tin roof at one time, but is now half covered in thatch.

There are eleven people living here and their surprise was almost equal to my own as I stepped out of the thick undergrowth. These are the first people I have seen in eleven days. They are probably BaNgwana people, and language is a bit of a problem as I can barely understand one word in a hundred when they talk to each other. However, with a lot of smiles and bits of Lingala, Swahili and French, accompanied by gestures and mime, we seem able to make some things understood – I think!

The little village has about seventeen banana trees and a patch of yams, which are being grown on mounds. There are two huge, buttressed trees, whose canopies overhang the clearing, and a good stream about thirty metres behind the yam patch. In other clearings nearby, the villagers have planted small crops of millet, maize and more yams.

Another of the village men returned just after my arrival. He had been hunting and had a duiker slung over his shoulder. His arrival revitalised the people's curiosity. Their welcome was obvious and I thought this an appropriate moment to produce the wild oranges I had collected earlier.

The villagers were delighted with my gift, but seemed much more interested in my bow and arrows. The man who had come back from hunting made approving noises over the plaited raffia bowstring and examined my arrows with a critical eye. By his manner, it was evident that he was trying to tell me something, but I completely failed to understand his meaning. Our earlier mixture of languages and mime was not up to the job.

Supper, which was eaten when evening came, consisted of hot soup, meal cakes with small bits of fruit in them, and grilled lumps of duiker meat. It was a wonderful feast, including the first meat I had eaten for weeks.

The hunter who had bagged the duiker cleaned and prepared his trophy for cooking himself. He skinned the little buck through the neck, so as to make a watertight bag. After gutting the carcass, he made off to go and bury the intestines in the forest. Realising what he was going to do, I made signs indicating that I would like to have them and, giving me a rather curious look, he handed them over. He followed me with interest as I took them to the stream to wash them, and then laughed with delight when I squeezed the water out and began twisting the long thin tube into a tight string, eventually stretching it out between two saplings to dry. In response to the man's shouts, most of the other villagers came to look and examine my work with a critical eye. I found it strange that it should be so, but it really seemed as if the whole idea was new to them.

One of the men – I think his name is Mula – kept looking meaningfully at the bark carapace on my right arm. Eventually I let him inspect it and then cut the binding and removed it. My jungle bandage has been in place for some days and I thought that the wound could probably do with a clean. Heads crowded round as I removed the bark and there was a great sucking of teeth and shaking of heads as my arm was finally revealed.

The wound was clean enough, but surrounded by an angry red swelling that started to throb as soon as the pressure of the bandage was removed. A great discussion began, with everyone offering their comments and asking questions, all of which were unintelligible to me. After a while, some of the women disappeared down a path to return a few minutes later with bunches of assorted leaves. These were passed from hand to hand and carefully inspected by everyone else, with leaves that were unsuitable for some reason or other being torn from the bunch and discarded as it was passed round. Eventually, a final selection was made. Ground between two stones, the chosen leaves were soon reduced to a pungent smelling green paste. A selection of berries were ground and mixed with the leaf paste, which was again passed round for inspection and comment.

Water was brought from the stream and my arm was washed. The salve was applied and a new bark carapace was bound on, with serious nods and approving comments from the watching villagers.

I noticed with some interest that the bark used for the new bandage was of the same variety as that which I had used the first time. This cheered me, as it suggested I had made at least one wise choice since I started out.

When supper was ready, some of the men started humming. This soon led to singing and as people finished eating they began to dance. A small drum was produced and soon everyone, including me, had joined in. The party lasted long into the night.

17th February. I woke to the pounding of the communal grain mortar. Two women were in action, lifting their heavy pestles high and bringing them down into the hollowed log with a rhythmic double thump. A girl I had not seen before was standing watching them, with her back to me. She was naked but for a waistband with a flap of grey cloth hanging in front and behind. I wondered where she had come from. Were there other villages nearby, or had she just remained out of sight in one of the huts?

When she turned, I saw that she was no girl, but a woman of about twenty years. Her features were very different from the other villagers. Although she had a broad flat nose, she was otherwise fine-featured, almost delicate, with thin lips and short braided hair. She wore no ornaments and her skin was like chocolate velvet.

As I walked over, she stood up and turned, displaying conical breasts and a smooth round belly above her waist cord. She was of much smaller stature than the other village women, her head reaching just above the level of my waist. I realised instantly that this gorgeous woman must be a Pygmy.

She was shy and moved quietly behind the other women, but continued to watch me closely, with no sign of fear. Her smile dissolved into a fit of giggles as the two women pounding grain talked and kept pointing at their chins. My beard, which had grown quite long during my travels, appeared to be the source of all this mirth. Their mounting hilarity was infectious and they soon had me laughing with them.

A man called Balam – I think he is Mula's brother – came with his bow and indicated that he and some others were going hunting. Did I wish to go along with them? I collected my bow and four arrows and we set off across the stream.

It was several miles along well-trodden paths to Balam's favourite hunting ground. Within minutes of our arrival he shot a monkey. It was a species I had not seen before, with grey fur, a buff chest and a black spot on its forehead. It was an adult female and weighed about eight pounds.

There were other monkeys in the trees, so I took aim and shot at them. Needless to say, I missed and lost two arrows. Balam laughed at this, borrowed my knife, and swiftly made me five more. Just like that!

On the way back, we took a different route and visited a Pygmy encampment. This was a natural clearing, with leaf debris scattered about, along with the burned remains of a huge fallen tree. Seven small domed huts surrounded the clearing, with their entrances facing towards the centre. Balam indicated that I should wait while he went into the camp. He returned a few minutes later and gestured for me to follow him.

Four small men watched my approach with wide-eyed curiosity. One was sitting on an upturned petrol can, the others were standing close by. It took about ten minutes for their reserve to melt, during which time they talked quietly with Balam and occasionally gestured in my direction. I sat down on a log. When they smiled, I smiled back and they soon began to grin broadly. Their eyes seemed to brighten and their talk became animated, but I could not understand a single word.

At first, I failed to notice that other Pygmies had joined us, but over the space of about an hour another dozen or so people, including women and children, appeared from the surrounding forest. One little boy walked straight over to me and pulled my beard. I was so surprised that I fell off the log and everyone dissolved into hysterical laughter.

Again, my bow was subjected to detailed examination. It was well over a foot longer than those made by these laughing little men. My arrows were also longer and had simple, straight points. Understanding my curiosity, they brought some of their own to show me. These were short and straight, made of hard reeds with black wooden tips. The tips were obviously ebony, beautifully worked and very sharp, with different shapes for birds, monkeys and ground dwellers. As the men handled my bow and arrows there was a lot of mime and at last I understood. They were telling me that their weapons were more suited to the thick jungle. Mine were so big that they would get tangled up in the undergrowth in the places where they usually hunted. How right they were!

Eventually, Balam indicated his desire to go home and we left amid shouts and laughter and impromptu dancing. I felt like Gulliver in Lilliput and pinched myself several times to be sure that this wonderful experience was real.

Back at the BaNgwana village, the light was already fading as I sat down to write my notes, eager to record this incredible day. To my surprise, Mula produced a battered hurricane lamp and set it by me, suspended from a forked stick. He seemed to understand that by writing, I was recording my experiences, but showed no great curiosity. I was struck by how thoughtful and generous these people are. As I wrote, a monkey was being roasted over the fire. It smelled delicious.

20th February. Day seventeen of my precious thirty days. I left the BaNgwana village early yesterday and continued my trek, moving roughly W by NW. It is quite impossible to move in straight lines in this sort of country, but at least I have now learned how to move in the jungle without having to hack through every pace with my machete. The new method is far less tiring and I have made good progress.

I met some more Pygmies today. I had killed a big snake earlier and was sitting on a mud bank beside a small stream, cooking it, when three small men emerged from the bushes on the opposite bank and stood watching me. I realised they must have been watching me from cover for some time, although I had been completely unaware of their presence.

Their approach seemed friendly, but shy, and they only came close when I offered to share my meal. One man immediately vanished, but returned a few moments later with a string bag full of fruit. We were all soon smiling and laughing and sucking on tender meat and juicy fruit.

When we had finished our meal, the three men crossed the stream and indicated that they were leaving. A gesture of the head invited me to follow and they all smiled when I tipped water over the dying embers of my fire and crossed after them.

It was some distance to their camp. There were about a dozen in the group, including five beautiful children. As I sat down, two of the children immediately climbed all over me. Some of the adults told them off, but when I laughed and allowed one little boy to roll me over everybody joined in the fun and all of them were soon giggling, singing and dancing.

These friendly people seem incapable of taking anything seriously and are so naturally at home with the forest that it is easy to become entranced by them. I wonder how much longer they will be left to live like this. Not too long, I fear, since 'civilisation' will inevitably encroach and destroy their harmony and their environment.

Watching their behaviour, it seems to me that they treat the forest with a casual, loving respect. They live with, not in, Ituri. There is no sign of gratuitous destruction or waste; they simply take what is needed at the time and leave everything else for the next user.

Today produced a surprise. I discovered that the cloth these little people wear around their loins is not cloth at all, but a type of bark. This has been beaten between two logs, with frequent rinsing in the stream until it becomes as soft and pliable as coarse cotton cloth. It seems to be quite durable and is eminently practical in this hot, humid environment.

I am down to wearing just shorts and sandals now; my trousers split and the legs have been converted into loincloths by two of the women. One of my boots lost its sole and the other is being used as a collecting basket for berries. The rubber sole of my defunct boot produced dense black smoke when it was put on the fire and was very effective at keeping the night bugs away. The smell was awful, but there is a price to pay for everything, and nobody seemed to mind.

My notebook has been the source of great interest and is inspected by everyone present each time I write something in it. The camera was treated with great reserve, but after I had taken a picture of the huts in the camp I managed to trip and drop it in a stream, so no more pictures. Somehow I don't mind. It seems right that all I shall take from here is this notebook and my memories; that is enough. These people have no material possessions; they simply borrow what they need from the forest, as and when they need it. Why should I do anything different?

I have been watching the little group make a new hut. It is simple, easy and quick. A framework was first made of thin saplings bent over to form a dome shape and bound together with plant fibre and fine vines. Within half and hour, the frame was finished and bunches of huge glossy leaves were being tied on, starting at ground level. The Pygmies call these leaves 'mongongo'. They grow all over the place and are between thirty and forty centimetres long and twenty to thirty across, with a thick, tough spine and stalk. The *mongongo* leaves are leathery and remain fresh and flexible for a long time after they are picked, making the huts completely rainproof.

In the steamy heat of this jungle, everything that is not actually growing rots quite fast and these small huts probably last no more than a few months. That is probably long enough, for the Pygmies appear to move about quite a lot and have no need of more permanent structures. They have no artifacts and make no pots or baskets, as far as I am able to see. Their spears, bows and arrows and hunting nets are durable enough, but are simply discarded when they break and new ones are soon made. Several of the spears I have seen have good metal tips, presumably traded with the Negro tribes who live on the forest fringes. Most, however, have ebony and other iron-hard wooden tips. Many of the arrows have toasted bamboo heads, which are bound into the shafts with sinew or palm fibre, and are without flights. These are obviously not necessary as they do not have to travel far to their targets. In this part of the jungle it is seldom possible to see more than about eight metres, and often not even as far as that, so targets are usually at very close range.

The spears are seldom longer than the owner is tall, often less, and are probably used more for stabbing than for throwing. The arrows are less than sixty centimetres long, being just shorter than an unstrung bow. These bows are made from very springy, quite hard wood, two and a half centimetres thick at the middle and tapered to half that towards each end. The bowstrings are made of gut or flat bark strips, bound on tightly to one end of the bow with a loop and notch at the other end. These Pygmies also make fine snares with vine fibres and are very adept at setting them.

My attempts to shoot a monkey caused great amusement, and will no doubt be talked about for a long time. We saw a troop of green monkeys in the trees and I shot at one that was sitting on a branch, grooming itself, no more than twenty feet away. I missed, of course, and my arrow stuck in the branch beside the monkey. The animal jumped and screeched with indignation at the impact, then snapped off the shaft and hurled it straight back at me. It was so funny that nobody else loosed an arrow and my little companions, delighted with this insult, literally fell about on the forest floor, hooting with laughter and kicking their legs in the air. We all ended up dancing round in circles, laughing and yelling and slapping each other on the back while the monkey retreated out of range into the dark upper reaches of the forest canopy.

It had been just too comical, the monkey wearing such an affronted look on his face. Every time the laughter started to subside, one or other of the Pygmies would leap up and shriek, imitating the sound and miming the actions of the event. At this everyone would collapse again in near hysterics.

I very soon realised that it was going to take a long time to live this one down, if I ever could. Never mind, they just make fun out of everything and everybody. One cannot possibly take offence, even when one is the butt of all the hilarity. It is quite wonderful.

1st March. Only five days left. There I go again, keeping track of time when these happy people are so totally spontaneous.

I said farewell and left their camp today, following a big game trail. Before I left, some of the men took me out and showed me an okapi. As we crept silently through the undergrowth, I found I was holding my breath in case it made a noise. After a while, excited gestures and flicking fingers drew my attention. I followed the pointing fingers, but could see only the greens, browns and dappled shadows of the dense thicket. Try as I might, I simply could not see what it was that they were trying to show me. My look of puzzled enquiry was too much for one of my companions and he began to laugh. Only then did the animal move, and I caught the briefest glimpse of it charging off. It had been less than three metres from me.

I saw another okapi later, but it did not have the same magic. It had been caught in a net by another group of Pygmies and had a broken leg. They seemed reluctant to kill it and I left hoping that it might survive and be released, although knowing that this was unlikely. It was an old animal and they probably ate it in the end.

4th March. I have now been on my own again for two-and-a-half days, travelling south west as fast as I am able in the hope of picking up one of the few 'roads' that exist in this area.

Travel has been easier for these few days and I have been following a larger river. I have no idea which river this is as they are not all marked on my map and most of those that are shown are not named. Anyway, I am hopeful that following it downstream should take me in the general direction in which I want to go. The forest here is a bit more open and I have passed several small cultivated patches, without actually encountering their owners or finding any settlements.

My injured arm has healed well, and there is hardly any sign of the deep gash that required my forest bandage. The herbal paste applied by the forest women has been remarkably effective and I wonder if modern western medicine could have done quite as well in this fetid environment.

I must keep moving as I am supposed to meet up with Bartolomée in two days time and get back to work. I still have no idea where I am.

6th March. People! I came across a small village and was guided the last few miles to a road. Apparently, the river I have been following is called the Aruwimi and the town of Banalia is only a few hours' walk to the south. I hope to be able to find a truck that is heading in the right direction as I am way off course, two hundred kilometres from where I need to be. I hope Bartolomée is patient and will wait for me.

The most immediate problem that I face is that of crossing this river. I am on the northern bank, but my route forward lies on the other side, and the only bridge has been washed out by flood water. The river is flowing deep and fast and there is no ferry. As there do not seem to be any canoes here, the only solution is to swim across. I bought a large, tightly woven basket in the market for just a few pence, in the hope that it will float long enough for me to keep what remains of my kit dry and get it over to the other side. The villagers tell me that the river is wider and not so deep upstream, so it should be easier to cross.

Stripped down to my shorts – I haven't much else to wear now, as it happens – and with my passport, camera, money and notebooks in a plastic bag inside the basket, I plan to take to the water, hoping that there are no hungry crocodiles about!

Well, I made it to the other bank without incident. In fact, it was easier than expected as I was able to wade more than two thirds of the way across and only had to swim for about thirty metres. Once I was back on the road, it did not take too long to reach Banalia, which turned out to be a scruffy little town, mostly made up of thatched huts and shacks built from flattened oil drums. There are a few more solid buildings, but even they have seen better days.

7th March. Walking through the town, I was hailed by an old French nun called Sister Dominique Lalande, who invited me to visit her mission. She told me that they have a vehicle going down to Kisangani, on the Congo River, on Monday and that I would be welcome to go with it if no transport is available before then. I have the feeling she knows there won't be anything before then. 180km to go.

On arrival at the mission, I was offered a hot bath and a good lunch. It felt strange to be sitting at a table, eating with a knife and fork, off china plates and in the company of four nuns. They are most hospitable and very informative about the local area and its people. They asked a lot of questions about my trip through Ituri. None of them have ever been into that region, although they have all been here for at least fifteen years.

The nuns have a problem with their generator and have asked me to see if I can do anything about it. I am not much of a mechanic, and even less of an electrician, but it seems churlish not to try, so I have agreed to have a go and have accepted their offer of transport on Monday.

This is a very tranquil place and it will be pleasant to relax for a day or so after the last five weeks of arduous travel. Even so, I feel slightly sad to have left the Ituri forest and its delightful, carefree people. They are free spirits, unburdened by the material world.

I, too, seem to have survived quite well with almost nothing – except a little help here and there from the people I met along the way. My kit has diminished significantly and now comprises: one ruined rucksack (thrown in the mission rubbish pit), a good basket and a tough plastic bag, the shorts, shirt and sandals I am wearing, two pairs of pants, a knife and machete, my match tin with six matches remaining, a defunct camera and films, two notebooks and half a pencil, my passport and 70 Zaïres in cash. I have spent the equivalent of 60 pence in the last three weeks!

Looking through my kit like this, I realize that I left my bow and single remaining arrow on the bank of the Aruwimi River. It's too late to go back for it now, and it seems rather appropriate that since I no longer have need of it, it should be returned to the forest from which it came.

Next, I must investigate the generator. The nuns have an excellent toolkit, but the man who normally wields it is away somewhere.

8th March. I was up to my elbows in oily machinery when a Landrover arrived and a familiar voice called out. Bartolomée had arrived early at our rendezvous, heard on the bush telegraph that there was a '*mundele ya barba*' in Banalia and so came up on the off chance.

His arrival was most fortuitous because he is a good mechanic and understands generators. He laughed at my efforts and, with the two of us working together, it took less than an hour to reassemble everything and get it running.

The nuns are delighted after three weeks without power. They refused my offer to pay for my lodging and food, saying that the return of their light is a far better payment. It is a curious facet of human nature that those who have the least are invariably the most generous.

9th March. This is to be my final entry in the diary. It is time to leave here and go back to work; the end of five uniquely glorious weeks spent trekking alone through the mysterious Mountains of the Moon and the magical Ituri Forest. Along the way, I encountered peoples and enjoyed experiences that very few others will ever be privileged to savour in quite the same way – my own personal Odyssey, never to be forgotten.

Footprints In The Dust

Boniface U'Ela worked as a sales assistant in the Church Missionary Society bookshop in Zaria, Northern Nigeria, and had a passion for natural history. When I went into the shop one day in search of a book on West African snakes, I discovered a kindred spirit and instantly made a new friend.

At fifteen, Boniface was about the same age as myself, had been educated at the local Anglican mission school. He had hopes of progressing to further study and eventually to some form of work involved with his country's wildlife. He came from a village about fifty miles east of Zaria, where his father had a farm. Boniface had a large family including three very pretty sisters. On my second visit to the bookshop, he introduced me to his friend Tuesday.

Tuesday Molosi had been educated at the same mission school, knew Boniface well and was a year older than me. He worked as a mechanic in the cotton mill that was located a few hundred yards beyond the bookshop and hoped one day to become the plant engineer. He was one of six brothers and came from a village only a few miles from the old mud-walled city. His father, Mfweza, was a potter and a pious man. He had named his first four sons, who were born at precise yearly intervals, after the four gospel writers – Matthew, Mark, Luke and John. For his fifth son, born more than three years after John, he had chosen the name Daniel, on the grounds that joining a family of four rumbustuous older brothers would be a bit like being thrown into a lion's den. By the time his sixth son arrived, Mfweza Molosi seemed to have run out of apposite biblical names. He called the boy Tuesday because that was the day on which he was born.

Boniface, Tuesday and I soon became good friends and when the other two were not at work, the three of us often spent time together, exploring the bush beyond the city or searching the dry river bed for amethysts, which were quite common in the area. One summer, we went with some other local lads to an agricultural fair that was being held in a village out beyond the university campus. It was only about six miles away and not too far to walk, but Tuesday somehow contrived to get us a ride most of the way on an overloaded mammy wagon called 'No Telephone to Heaven'.

Mammy wagons are the standard freight vehicle of West Africa. Always overloaded, they are usually aged trucks that have been repaired and modified so many times as to be completely unrecognisable to the original manufacturer's engineers. They all have picturesque names painted on a board above the driver's cab and usually have a crowd of at least twenty people perched on top of the freight together with their goats, baskets of chickens, bags of grain and all sorts of other domestic possessions or market goods. These vehicles are known as mammy wagons partly because most of their passengers are usually women, but also because most of them are actually owned by women, who are the principals of most of West Africa's market trade. 'No Telephone to Heaven' was one I came to know well over the next three and a half years. Tragically, it came to a dramatic end during the Nigerian civil war when it ran over a landmine and was blown to pieces, killing eleven people.

It had become a bit of a joke among us lads that the only white boy among us was more at ease in the African bush than his local black friends. That was where I had grown up and, as a result, I had learned how to use its resources from the earliest possible age. Whilst many of my friends had been born in villages, they had all moved to the towns and now only went into the hinterland when some family obligation or other pressing reason took them home. They had become more than a little wary of being in the wide open country, where game and predators roamed free, and were much more comfortable in the busy urban streets that had become their home. Because of my reputation as a hardened country boy, I should perhaps not have been surprised, therefore, when I found on arrival at the agricultural fair that my friends had had a whip round to raise the entrance fee of one pound and had entered me for a goat skinning competition.

A West African agricultural fair is not for the faint hearted – especially the goat skinning competition, which starts with live goats! Since I had been accustomed either to shooting my own meat or to buying it on the hoof, this did not particularly bother me. As well as a goat that was tethered to a stake, each contestant was given a knife and an enamel bowl. One look at the knife did bother me as it would not have cut a ripe pawpaw. I asked the judge for a few minutes to sharpen the blade before we began. He agreed and I went in search of a suitable stone. This caused a ripple of applause and some amusement as people watching shouted ribald comments. I noticed also that people were taking bets on the competition's outcome and wondered if any of my friends had had a bet on me. Among the other competitors I could see a man who sold meat in the Sabon Gari market and imagined he must be the favourite.

With my blade sharpened, I was ready to begin and the judge blew his horn. Blades sliced, blood flowed into bowls, goats twitched and died and their guts were spilled out on the ground like piles of thick macaroni. Within a couple of minutes, each of us was surrounded by a buzzing cloud of flies as we pulled and sliced to remove the skin from our carcasses. I had a lot less flies than anyone else since I had cut carefully and only opened the skin, leaving my goat's entrails undisturbed within the carcase. It took only a few minutes to remove the skin, stretch it and peg it out in the sun to dry. Before doing anything else with the goat, I made sure that the skin was clean and that all the fat had been removed. By the time I removed the entrails and started twisting the intestines to make string, I was aware of a very attentive audience around me. I kept working and tried to ignore them. I hung the heart and liver on the stake to which the goat had originally been tethered, blew up the bladder and secured it to dry as a useful bag, or maybe to be stuffed with grass and used as a football, and a few minutes later heard the judge's horn blow to signal the end of the competition.

It had been quite a busy session and I had no idea how long we had been working. As I stood up and looked around, I was more than a little surprised to see that several of the goats had still not had their skins completely removed. The next thing I knew, the judge was standing beside me, shaking my hand and congratulating me on being the winner! My friends were all leaping up and down, cheering and patting me on the back and Tuesday was waving a fistful of banknotes. Obviously somebody had had a bet on me and at good odds, too.

The Emir of Zaria, Alhaji Mohamadu Aminu, presented me with my prize, a crisp ten pound note. He asked me what I would do with it and I told him I would try to buy a horse.

"Have you seen one you like?" he enquired.

"Oh yes, Excellency," I said. "But I cannot afford that one. I know someone else who tried to buy her and the price was too high."

The Emir knew a lot about horses. He kept many himself and was president of both the local polo club and the Zaria Horse Racing Club. It was said that in his youth he had been a fine horseman, although he was now far too large and heavy to ride in either sport. But he still had a keen eye for a good beast.

"Which one is she, this costly animal?" he asked, looking over to where the horses were all gathered. I pointed out a pretty strawberry roan mare and he smiled.

"Ah, Halissa. She is one of mine," he said and I nodded agreement, for I already knew that. I also knew that he had recently refused an offer of four hundred pounds for her.

I was still holding the ten pound note he had given me a few moments before and suddenly he whisked the note out of my hand.

"Sold," he announced. "You have just bought a fine mare." He handed the banknote to his Waziri, who was always at his elbow, and snapped his fingers twice. "For eight pounds," he added, stuffing two grubby one pound notes into my hand.

"But.." I spluttered, not quite knowing what to say.

"Take good care of Halissa," he said. "I shall want to see her when I come to the barracks for the Independence Day parade." He turned away as if dismissing a minion, as kings are wont to do.

To his already retreating back I called out: "Thank you, Excellency. I will care for her as your own *doki-boy* would do."

'No Telephone to Heaven' had to go without our merry band that evening as, along with many others, we took the main road back towards Zaria, leading the strawberry roan. Everyone we passed seemed to have heard about the goat skinning competition and as many more knew that I had bought my mare from the Emir for a ridiculous price. This was seen as a mark of favour bestowed on me, and my friends basked in the reflected glory.

Word of my purchase had somehow preceded me and my parents came out to have a look at the mare when I arrived home. My Dad chuckled when he saw her and remarked that he knew someone who was going to be miffed when he found out. It was one of his Company Commanders at the barracks whose offer the Emir had turned down.

"If you want to play polo with her, I suggest you ask Ken to teach you," Dad advised. "He's very good and could help you a lot."

"Apart from which, he will probably knobble you the first time you're on an opposing team to him if you don't," added my mother. "Ken can be a mean spirited sod when he's upset – and this will definitely upset him."

"Thanks for the warning," I said. "I'll go and see him in the morning."

In fact, Ken wasn't too upset, but was obviously pleased that I had asked for his help. He turned out to be as good a teacher as he was a polo player and the mare responded excellently. He seemed even more pleased when I offered him the use of the mare for home games during school term time, when I would be back in the UK. Halissa progressed well with European tack, which is considerably kinder to the horse than the local bridle and saddle that she had on when I bought her.

Within a few months she had really shaped up well, but there were two things she hated, ditches and snakes, both of which made her stand up on her hind legs and paddle at the air with her front hooves. I occasionally took her out in the bush, but always made sure that we were either back home or safely inside a stock pen with other animals before nightfall. It was one thing being out in the bush myself at night, but I was not sure how some of the strange noises and smells might spook the mare.

For this reason, Halissa stayed in the stable when Boniface, Tuesday and I set off to spend a couple of days at Boniface's home village. Tuesday had been introduced to one of his sisters and was very keen to further the acquaintance. With all I had heard about Boniface's sisters, I was quite keen to meet them myself. On Friday morning we went down to the Sabon Gari market to the place from where all the mammy wagons and bush taxis started their journeys. We were lucky enough to find a mammy wagon that was intending to pass within a mile of Boniface's village. It would leave at one thirty. We wandered round the market for a while, collecting a few things to take for Boniface's family and were back at the wagon park with time to spare. Rather surprisingly, the truck left within a few minutes of the appointed time, with us and about twenty other people clinging to the top of the swaying cargo, which felt and smelt like sacks of dried stock fish.

Mammy wagons travel slowly and stop for the slightest excuse. They will also sometimes change their route or destination without notice, which is precisely what happened to us.

We had travelled some twenty miles when the truck suddenly turned right and headed south. Since we had seen no diversion signs this seemed rather odd and a number of passengers started banging on the cabin roof to attract the driver's attention. The vehicle lurched to a stop and an altercation ensued in which everyone seemed to be yelling at the same time. Silence was only restored when the driver gave a long blast on his air horns, a whole battery of which surmounted the cab. Eventually, we discovered that one of the passengers in the cab was a sister of the wagon's owner. This lady had decided, apparently on the spur of the moment, that she simply had to visit a friend who lived about thirty five miles south of where we were and had ordered the driver to take her there first before finding an alternative route on towards the original destination.

This seemed to present no great inconvenience to most of the other passengers, but we three didn't want to go that far out of our way and felt we had no choice but to part company with the truck. We demanded a refund of our fares and the owner's sister grudgingly threw a dirty ten shilling note in the dust and informed us that, as we had already travelled some distance, that was all she was prepared to give us by way of reimbursement. The driver immediately gunned his engine and drove off, leaving us standing beside the dusty road in a cloud of red laterite dust

"Do you know how much further it is, Boniface?" I asked.

"Maybe twenty five or twenty eight miles," he replied.

"Does the road go straight?" I asked.

"No, it goes this way for about another ten miles and then bends round to the left. He waved his arm to show us. " You can see a cleft in the hills up there. The road goes through that. We have to go about five or six miles more after that."

I looked at the sun. It would be down in about two and a half hours. If we headed directly towards the cleft in the hills we could probably save ourselves some miles. We had seen no other traffic on the road and it seemed unlikely that there would be any. We had blankets, a cooking pot, some food and a few other things with us, so I reckoned we might as well take the most direct route and camp somewhere for the night once it got dark. I proposed the idea, but the other two looked dubious.

"If either of you has a better idea, let's hear it," I concluded. They had to admit that my idea did make sense, and since they knew that I was used to the bush and would look after them, they eventually agreed. We picked up our baskets, perched them on our heads and set off, with me leading the way. Tuesday decided that if anyone was going to walk into an ant colony or step on a snake, he would rather it was me than him, so he would follow. Boniface thought that was an excellent notion and straggled behind. I noticed that he hurried to catch up when I laughingly suggested that whoever was at the rear might be in danger of getting his backside bitten by baboons, who were known to sneak up on unwary travellers in the bush.

At dusk, I selected a suitable spot to camp and we stopped. It did not take long to collect enough wood to make a fire and we found some dry thorny branches to protect us on three sides. I had chosen a spot near a small stream, with no obvious sign that it was a regular drinking spot for any of the more dangerous wild inhabitants of the region, so we used the stream to protect the fourth side and made ourselves comfortable. Among our supplies, we had brought a pot of cassava porridge as well as some fruit. We also had a lump of meat that we had bought in the Sabon Gari before boarding the mammy wagon. Tuesday sliced this up while Boniface built up the fire and I cut each of us a stick to use as a toasting fork. We then settled down for a meal under the stars.

It was the middle of the dry season, so there was no risk of rain. The Milky Way, unobstructed by urban light pollution, was a brilliant sparkling arc above us and the first quarter of the new moon added a clean, silver sheen to everything. We talked about the afternoon's adventures and, for the umpteenth time, Tuesday had Boniface tell him all about the sister he had introduced him to. Having heard at great length about all her virtues, I thought it was only fair that we should hear about the other two sisters as well. What else should young men talk about together under the stars, I asked myself? Pretty girls seemed like a perfect topic to me. Eventually, we began to tire and after I had built up the fire so that it would burn steadily, but not too fiercely all night, we wrapped ourselves in our blankets and lay down to sleep. At first, I lay watching the stars, but being close to a stream there were mosquitoes about, so I soon pulled the blanket over my head and closed my eyes. Sleep must have come quickly, but then I seldom have trouble falling asleep, even out in the open bush.

It must have been some time in the early hours that I was awoken by a soft rhythmic buzzing sound, almost like a cat purring. I lay still and listened, but could not decide precisely what it was. The usual night sounds had been suspended. The crickets that normally scrape their shrill song incessantly throughout the darkest hours of the night were unusually silent. The squeak of bats that had periodically punctured the quiet when I first lay down was stilled and even the rustle of tiny rodents in the scrub was absent. Only one thing could cause this silence, the presence of a major predator.

My attention was drawn back to the soft buzzing sound. I wondered briefly if there was a swarm of bees or other insects settling in the tree above me, but the sound seemed to come and go rather like something breathing in and out. It also seemed to be moving around, steadily and quite slowly. First it came from one side and then the other, almost as if it were working its way round our little camp. I was just making up my mind to pull the blanket from my head and have a look when I heard what sounded like a low cough between where I lay and the fire. The purring sound increased in volume and appeared to come nearer. Then it was above my head. I heard something sniffing and could smell the rank odour of its breath. Now I knew that some animal had breached our basic perimeter and was looking round our camp, right beside me and unafraid of the fire. I wondered if it was a large bull baboon and decided that inertia was probably my best protection. It was possibly my only protection and I sincerely hoped my two friends were still soundly asleep.

After a few moments the animal moved away from my head and I could almost feel it sniffing at my crotch. It was still making the purring noise when I felt something tickle my right heel. With horror, it dawned on me that my blanket must have ridden up, leaving my foot exposed. A moment later, I became paralysed with fright as something that felt like wet sand-paper cloth was dragged across the sole of my foot. My instinct was to scream and pull up my foot, but good sense, and the clamping of my jaws tight on my own tongue, overcame my panic and kept me still.

The purring sound diminished and moments later there was a rustle followed by a low cough, the crack of snapping twigs and a sharp squeal of agony. A moment later, I heard more twigs snapping and branches rustling as if something was being dragged through them, followed by silence.

I lay still for quite a while, not sure whether whatever it was had departed completely. A few minutes later there was another squeal that was abruptly cut off, as if some small animal had been caught and killed. After another short interlude, the deathly silence eased as crickets again resumed their scraping song. An owl screeched somewhere off among the trees and a nightjar called. The night was back to normal. Our visitor had gone.

Softly I called to the others: "Are you awake?"

"Yes," two frightened voices answered almost simultaneously. "What was that?"

"We had a visitor who was not afraid of the fire," I said, pulling my blanket down and looking towards the orange embers. There were no flames now, but the orange glow was still bright, the smell of wood smoke pungent on the cool night air. I reached over and pushed another couple of thick sticks into the hot embers. In a moment they caught and small flames danced, shedding a small pool of yellow light, but not enough to see much by. I kept my hand on the end of one of the burning sticks, ready to take hold and use it as a weapon. We lay, awake and still, until the rising sun lightened the eastern sky and finally spilled its brilliance over the line of hills we had been walking towards the previous afternoon.

Darkness comes rapidly in Africa. Day dawns as quickly and within fifteen minutes of the first golden rays peeping over the rim of hills the land was bathed in warm golden light and the cool of the night was giving way to the early morning heat of another roasting, burnished day. I pulled off my blanket and stood up, looking around the place where I had been lying.

The soft dust was spotted all around with footprints. Our visitor had made a circuit of the fire and of each one of us in turn as we lay, helpless. I could clearly see where the beast had paused by my head and again at my feet. It must have been a long white whisker that had tickled my heel. I could imagine the huge fanged teeth that would have surrounded the tongue that had rasped across the sole of my foot, and my blood ran cold again.

The marks were the biggest leopard prints I had ever seen. The great spotted cat had examined each one of us carefully. It had licked my foot and may have been about to take a bite when it had been distracted by something else. Broken twigs and a small pool of blood on the far bank of the stream revealed where it had charged off and seized some poor, unsuspecting animal that strayed into its hunting zone. After a few moments tracking, I found a small hoof, dropped from the cat's impromptu meal. It was the hind hoof of a duiker, a small cat-sized deer that would have been little more than a mouthful for the leopard. A few yards further on, I found where its mate had also met its end. That must have been the second squeal I had heard. It was our good fortune that the pair of duiker had come along, for the leopard is the only one of the big cats that will strike for fun. The others hunt only when they are hungry, but the leopard is a mean beast and enjoys playing with its prey, which it will then store in a tree for several days before eating. We had been incredibly lucky.

As we made a hasty breakfast on the leftovers of the previous night's meal, the others asked me about our visitor. They both looked around anxiously when I told them what it had been. I showed them where it had entered our camp, where it had paused and how it had left in pursuit of the diminutive antelope that had replaced us on the menu.

"I knew it was trouble when we found that mammy wagon," Tuesday said. "We should have abandoned the trip before we started."

"Why?" Boniface and I asked in unison.

"Didn't you see the mammy wagon's name?" asked Tuesday. "It was called 'No Hurry To Die' and it was painted with black dots on a yellow board. It made me think."

It made us all think as we hurried to break camp and headed on towards Boniface's village. About a mile after we left our camp, I saw something in the lower branches of a flat-topped acacia tree and steered towards it to take a closer look. We didn't need to get too close to recognise it as our nocturnal visitor, now dozing after his night's exertions. I pointed him out to Boniface and Tuesday who immediately started to walk faster.

Needless to say, when we got to the village the story underwent all sorts of embellishment in Tuesday's and Boniface's recounting. I was still feeling slightly embarrassed at the terror I had felt and left most of the telling to them. Boniface's three sisters turned out to be endowed with even more than the extensive virtues their brother had told us about. They made a good audience and were enthusiastic in their appreciation of Tuesday's theatrical portrayal of the night's events. I could well understand why he was interested in the eldest of the three and it was quite apparent that his interest was reciprocated.

We enjoyed our visit and promised to come again soon. On

Monday morning we got up early and headed off towards the junction with the road where 'No Hurry To Die' should have dropped us on Friday. The villagers told us that there was always more traffic at the beginning of the week and we should have no trouble getting a ride. Even so, the others were not taking any risk of being stranded overnight in the bush again.

We reached the junction and started along the road back towards the old city, leaving a trail of footprints behind us in the dust to be erased by the first vehicle that happened along. Looking back, I could not help remembering the other dusty footprints we had so recently left behind us.

We had been walking for almost an hour when a mammy wagon came up behind us and slowed as we waved to ask for a ride. It was our old friend 'No Telephone To Heaven' and her driver had news that was both unwelcome and at the same time a tremendous relief to us. He told us that another wagon, 'No Hurry To Die', had hit a large rock the previous night and had rolled over, killing seventeen people who had been riding on top and four in the cab. The wreck caught fire and had been completely destroyed.

The Headman's Dilemmas

Mawokumiu, headman of Asokoné for over sixty-five years, was the father of the village in a very real sense. Still vigorous and active at the age of one hundred and two, he had married one hundred and sixteen wives, eighty-two of whom were still alive. Of the many hundreds of children that these wives had borne him over the years, three hundred and forty-eight had survived the ravages of infancy in the African bush and had reached adulthood.

These, in turn, had so far delivered him five hundred and sixty-seven grandchildren who had generated a further four hundred and eighty-two great-grandchildren. And since girls are married and start breeding soon after puberty in such rural areas, it is hardly surprising that Mawokumiu's progeny also included eleven great-great-grandchildren.

The total number of his direct descendants thus amounted to one thousand, four hundred and eight. Not all the members of this vast extended family still lived in Asokoné; some of the girls had married men from other villages and had moved away. However, Asokoné remained their home village and most of them returned with their spouses to visit relatives and to participate in significant festivals and events. Equally, some of Mawokumiu's sons had married girls from other villages and had brought them home to live in Asokoné. The result of all this was that out of a total population in 1971 of over one thousand there were only about two hundred who were not directly descended from Mawokumiu.

Effectively, the headman was the law in the village. The Government was little more than a minor and remote factor in their lives. In this isolated rural corner of northern Cameroon, few government officials were in post and even fewer were ever seen in the villages. Not that the villagers took any serious notice of them when they did visit. They were usually viewed as novelties, surrounded by crowds of chattering children and stared at by the adults in that blank, speculative way that reveals nothing of what is going on in minds that are actually absorbing every little detail of what is said and done and storing it all away in preparation for vigorous discussion later, when the strangers have departed.

From their former colonial masters, the villagers had long ago learned the art of apparent compliance. They would make a token show of doing what the officials demanded when they visited, only to revert to their own ways as soon as these officials had gone. As a result, the government had little effect on lives that were ordered according to time-honoured local traditions and a rich, complex system of tribal taboos and customs. These were overseen and enacted through the inherited authority of the village elders and the headman and through the constant cycle of arcane practices and rituals performed by the local witch doctor.

Since the area was so remote, with few roads and none of the convenient facilities and services of more urban communities, very few outsiders were willing to remain there for any length of time. Indeed, on the rare occasions when they did visit, the government officials, all of whom were townsfolk from the south, stayed only as long as they needed to and then hurried back to the comforts of civilisation. The only government building in the area had long since fallen into dereliction and now stood empty and unused, in glorious isolation over half a mile down the mountain, below the village.

In late June, word had gone round the village that strangers were coming, but nothing happened. Rumours persisted that strangers had been seen in some of the other villages in the area, but nobody could offer a clear description or say who they were. Mawokumiu consulted the witch doctor and asked for a divination. That was not necessary, the shaman told him, since this event had long been foreseen and the timing was now right. A new man was coming to live among them.

"But who is he? And why is he coming?" the headman demanded.

"You will see," was all the witch doctor would say, as he shuffled uncomfortably on his stool.

A few days later, an old and battered Peugeot pick-up grumbled its way up the steep track, weaving in and out of the scrubby trees and scraping its dull paint on the hard red earth castles of the many termite mounds that littered the slope. The back of the vehicle was piled high with boxes and bales, on top of which were lashed lengths of sawmill timber, topped by sheets of bright new wriggly tin.

The driver was a short, thin white man, deeply sun tanned, with a dense thatch of iron grey hair. Beside him was a stout little woman of indeterminate age. She had a round smiling face and her hair was tied up behind her head in a tight bun.

The people of Asokoné heard the approaching vehicle long before it became visible. As soon as they realised there was something coming, all the children hurried off to have a look. Most of them had never seen a motor vehicle since there was no proper road to the village, merely a narrow track that wound up the mountainside.

At first, the children peered nervously from behind rocks and anthills, careful in case this growling monster, which by this time had a damaged exhaust and therefore made a great deal of noise, might be dangerous. To them, the sound of the engine, although much louder, was not unlike that of the lions and leopards they often heard roaring and coughing in the bush.

When she spied the inquisitive faces watching from their vantage points, the woman in the vehicle smiled and waved at them, calling out greetings that were drowned by the noise of the engine. Before long, the children lost their timidity and came out to surround the slowly moving vehicle, smiling, chattering and shouting to the visitors who, of course, could hear nothing over the deafening noise of the un-silenced exhaust. As the pick-up mounted the slope and drew nearer to the village, the accompanying crowd rapidly swelled until, soon, almost half the population was escorting the visitors.

After an hour of laborious progress, the ancient Peugeot heaved itself over the gritty shoulder of the mountain onto a small plateau where the remains of the old government building stood in lonely and dejected isolation. The roof had collapsed and the once white walls were now flaking and in need of major repairs. The wooden door had long ago been ravaged by termites. A pair of rusting hinges, lying on the ground nearby, was the only evidence that a door had ever been there.

The driver stopped on the flat space in front of the ruined building and turned off the engine. The sudden silence stilled the voices of the surrounding crowd, who watched expectantly as the doors opened and the occupants emerged from the scratched and dented cab.

The silence was short lived. A child's voice called out a greeting and there was general amazement when the white man replied, loud and clear, in the same dialect. Within moments, others were calling out and the new arrivals responded as they approached, hands outstretched in greeting.

The crowd absorbed them like an amoeba, and the milling tide carried the visitors back to the village to be presented to the headman. After a cursory inspection of the laden pick-up, even the children followed, leaving the vehicle unattended and becalmed outside the broken building.

Mawokumiu was not in the village when the crowd reached his house. He was out in the fields with some of his wives, watching as they harvested yams. A messenger arrived with news of the visitors' arrival, but having questioned the boy closely, the old man returned his attention to the task in hand. Only when enough tubers had been dug up to satisfy his household did he show any interest in returning to the village. Even then, he insisted on stopping by a stream for half an hour to wash himself before eventually heading home.

He chose a route that enabled him to approach his house from the back, giving him the opportunity to observe the visitors for a few minutes, unseen, before meeting them. He found them seated in the courtyard, chatting to the assembled crowd. They were discussing the differing merits of keeping chickens and ducks with their hosts, whilst drinking from a calabash of millet beer that was being passed round.

When the witch doctor had first confirmed that strangers were coming, it had never occurred to Mawokumiu that they might be white men. It was so many years since he had last seen a white man that he had all but forgotten that they existed. He was, therefore, slightly startled to see two white people being entertained by his wives and children. His surprise was all the greater on hearing them speak his language so fluently as, in his previous experience, few white people bothered to learn the indigenous tongue. They usually expected the people to learn their coarse words and berated them for being stupid and not trying properly when they found the words hard to pronounce and the grammar incomprehensible.

Before making an appearance, Mawokumiu sent word to his witch doctor to ask what manner of people these might be. The answer came back saying simply that these were the visitors whose coming had been foretold, and nothing more. It occurred to him for the first time that the outside world had seen some big changes since he had last been away from home and that, maybe, that new world was now coming closer. If they had come to stay, these people could be the harbingers of a whole new era for his community.

He was both excited and slightly afraid as he emerged to take his place on his ceremonial Stool of Dignity in front of the assembled villagers and intoned the formal words of greeting that bid his visitors welcome.At a signal from the headman, food was brought and more calabashes of beer were passed round. The visitors seemed both familiar and comfortable with the customs, unlike the whites Mawokumiu had met so many years before, most of whom were nervous and tense. These people chatted openly with all who spoke to them and were as willing to tell about themselves as they were to hear what the villagers had to say. They were as friendly and accepting of the children's and others' attention as they were respectful towards the headman and the village elders.

Alexander McKenzie introduced himself to the village and their headman, informing them that he had come with his wife, Sheila, to live here and bring the people the teachings of God.

"Which god?" someone asked.

"There is only one," he said.

"But we know many," he was told.

"Those that you know are different faces of the same one. There is only one God," he replied gently, but very definitely.

"How can this be?" another villager asked.

McKenzie glanced at the headman and received his nod of consent before responding. Then he began his ministry and delivered his first sermon to the people of his new parish.

While he was talking, his wife walked back to their vehicle with a small escort of children and one or two of the younger women. She returned some time later bearing a bale of cloth, topped by a large oblong basket. These she had balanced on her head, carrying the heavy load just as the village women would do.

The missionary was just completing his sermon as she wove her way through the throng of villagers and deposited her basket at his feet. She placed the bale of bright cloth on top of the basket and sat down on the ground beside her load. Her manner and demeanour matched those of an African wife, a point that was observed with interest by the headman and the elders.

After the sermon was over, McKenzie opened the basket and distributed some gifts to Mawokumiu and the elders. When he had finished, his wife unwrapped the bale of printed cotton cloth. This had already been divided into generous lengths, with several different colour schemes and patterns. She gave one piece to each of the adult women.

The gifts were received with cries of delight as the people festooned themselves with their trophies. The children were not forgotten, for the basket also contained small garments and strings of bright beads that were accepted with great enthusiasm.

McKenzie explained to the headman that they had bought the old government building and that they were going to rebuild it as a church. It would become a happy place, he promised, full of singing and joy and learning; a place where everyone would be welcome. Once that work was complete, he would, if the headman permitted, build himself a small house nearby.

The news was received with a casual gesture of acceptance from the headman, whose curiosity had been piqued by things he had heard in the newcomer's sermon. He needed to know more, so as to be better equipped to guide his people. In his long lifetime, Mawokumiu had seen many changes. He realised that the march of progress was inevitable and that the secret for survival was to be prepared for what was coming. He saw, too, that the arrival of these interesting strangers represented a turning point in the history of his community that he could not ignore.

Later that afternoon, the McKenzies unloaded their pick-up, pitched a tent beside the derelict building and set up home. The next morning, they rose early and started work on clearing all the collapsed debris from the ruin. The remains of the old thatch were pulled out and burned, the crumbling blocks that had fallen when part of the walls collapsed were scraped up and carried away and the rotten remains of rafters, windows and door frames were pulled out and added to the pile of old wood that was to fuel Sheila McKenzie's cooking stove in their first few weeks.

At first the McKenzies worked alone, but after a few hours some of the village men came and lent a hand. McKenzie started a chant and before long all the workers were singing lustily and the work gathered pace. Up in the village, Mawokumiu heard the raised voices. The white man had told him the repaired building would be full of songs and happiness. It seemed he was indeed a man of his word.

The clearing up was completed before sunset and it was a happy band of villagers who gathered their children and returned to their houses as darkness fell.

The old Peugeot's load had included a small hydraulic block press. This was put to good use during the next few days, making enough mud blocks to repair the broken walls. The blocks were laid out in long lines in the sun to dry and to receive the critical inspection of the village artisans. While they were curing, McKenzie prepared the timber he had brought to make new rafters for the church roof. Cutting each piece to size and numbering it, he laid them all out in a carefully planned pattern on the other side of the building from the lines of blocks.

They worked for six days and on the seventh they rested. On that morning, people who had come down from the village expecting to work were treated instead to offerings of tea and fresh baked bread while McKenzie delivered them his second sermon. Somehow, nobody objected to this talk, as what he said made good sense to them. He had talked frequently about God while they were working together during the week, linking every activity to examples from the customs and practices of the people. What he now said served merely to give strength to their own beliefs while drawing them together under one supreme deity.

During the following week, the walls were repaired and whitened with lime, inside and out. The windows were replaced with new, brightly painted shutters, and a new wide, arched front door was installed. Clay was brought up from the river valley to resurface the floor, which was then beaten smooth and burnished. And all the while McKenzie kept talking to the villagers, telling them stories that linked their ways with the holy message he had come to deliver. They, in turn, worked with enthusiasm and joined in the new songs he taught them with gusto. Almost everyone in the village participated in some part of the work, although they still maintained their own fields and carried out all their other regular daily activities.

The third week was spent making many more mud blocks and laying them out to cure in the sun. There seemed to be enough for a whole new building and some people wondered if these were for the house McKenzie had said he was going to build. But others pointed out that he had said he would not begin building his house until the church had been completed. He had always been a man of his word so there must be some other purpose for these extra blocks.

Speculation increased when Sheila McKenzie collected grass and started weaving long narrow strips of thick springy matting. The village women joined in and the pile of completed mats grew rapidly. The mats were plain at first, but then Sheila wove in a coloured pattern and soon all the mats were being decorated with ever more intricate designs. Like her husband, Sheila McKenzie told stories as she worked and taught the women the same songs that the men had been singing.

As the days rolled by, Mawokumiu sat in his compound,

hearing accounts of what was going on from the members of his family who had joined in the work and listening to the cadence of the singing that periodically wafted up the slope to the village. His interest grew, and each evening he quizzed his sons on what McKenzie had been talking about during the day.

He, too, was curious to know what all the extra blocks were for when, according to what his sons told him, it appeared that the walls were already complete. The grass mats also offered scope for interesting speculation.

During the fourth week, McKenzie used the new blocks to build a tower against the back wall of the building. When the tower was twice the height of the other walls, McKenzie called a halt. A lattice of woven sticks was laid across the open top, covered with a thick, closely woven mat and then plastered with clay, which was burnished to a smooth glossy finish as it dried. McKenzie used most of his remaining timber to make a strong frame that was hoisted up to sit on top of the tower, with a stout rope hanging from one corner.

That night, after the villagers had gone home, McKenzie climbed the tower and hauled up a heavy package, wrapped in sacking. After only a few minutes work, a large brass bell was suspended on a spindle in the middle of the frame. A thin rope was then passed through a small hole in the smartly plastered roof. Finally, the top of the rope was attached to an arm on the bell, while the bottom was allowed to fall free inside the tower.

That done, he fetched a folding table from his tent and placed it in front of the back wall inside the church. Covering it with a cloth, he placed a simple wooden cross upright on the table and then helped his wife to bring in all the grass mats, laying them out in rows across the floor.

Looking around, the couple admired all the work that their new friends had done. In less than a month they had taken a derelict shell and made it whole and beautiful. Their church was now ready for use.

Early in the morning, Sheila McKenzie went through the narrow doorway into the tower. She pulled rhythmically on the rope, tolling the bell to invite the villagers to church.

Of course, everyone came to investigate the unfamiliar noise. McKenzie stood at the open door, welcoming people as they arrived and inviting them in to sit on the grass mats. When the bell had tolled a hundred and two times, it stopped. McKenzie went into the church as his wife emerged from the tower.

That day he conducted his first service in God's new house. It started with the singing of a song he had taught people while they were working on the building and they all joined in lustily. He then recited prayers that picked out spirits recognised by the villagers and wove them in as parts of the one special being he had first told them about; and he gave them another rousing sermon that explained how the quality of the work they had done on the church was a reflection of their offerings to God.

McKenzie told the villagers that although the church was God's house, the door would always be open, and everyone would be welcome there at any time. It was a place for the people to praise God's gifts to them; to tell God of their concerns and seek guidance and help; it was a place of happiness, where disagreements should be left outside the door so that those who entered would do so in peace to heal their differences. He had promised them it would also be a place of learning and now that the building was done, he would start the very next day to teach all those who wanted to learn, particularly the children.

When McKenzie went into the church the following morning, the place was already crowded. All the village children and many of the younger adults were there, seated in rows, waiting quietly. Even one or two of the older folk had come. He had not foreseen a response like this. In fact he had only dared hope for a dozen or so pupils, but here were over two hundred people eager to find out what school was about.

Some weeks after the McKenzies started their school, a man claiming to be a government official arrived in the village. He had evidently not been told that the former government building had been sold and he was furious to find it being used as a church by a white man whom he instantly disliked and despised. He was loud and forceful in his protests and became even more irate as a crowd of villagers gathered to watch the encounter. McKenzie tried to reason with him and even showed him the official bill of sale, but the government man did not even bother to read this. Snatching it from McKenzie's hand, he screwed it up, threw it on the ground and stamped on it, yelling insults and threats.

The crowd jeered and one or two raised sticks as if to beat the man. He merely increased his threats and demanded that the headman must expel this foreigner from the village or else he would have to bring the police to do it. The villagers jeered again, but opened a way through the crowd so that the official could go up to the village to confront their headman.

Word had already gone back to the village about what was afoot, so the headman had been warned and was prepared. When the government official reached the chief's compound he found the gate firmly shut. A single white egret feather was stuck in the ground before it, with a dark kite feather a few inches behind. The official stopped in his tracks and stared at the sign. He said nothing, though the look on his face betrayed the boiling anger that seethed within him.

The villagers had never seen a sign such as this and fell silent to watch what the government man would do. He did nothing for several long minutes, but simply stared furiously at the closed gate. At length he sat down beside the gate, leaned his back against the compound wall and settled down to wait, ignoring those who watched him.

All afternoon he waited, but the gate remained closed. As dusk fell, the villagers began to lose interest and started gradually drifting away to their homes. At dawn, the government man was still seated beside the gate, waiting, when the first curious villagers arrived. The sun was already high in its arc when one of Mawokumiu's sons opened the gate, removed the planted feathers and indicated that the official could enter.

The man's belligerence had not been diminished by the enforced wait and he strode into the compound like an invading warrior. He was surprised to find the place full of villagers and the elders already in discussion, with the white man and his woman seated among the onlookers. The disapproval on the government man's face was clear to everyone as he marched towards the headman, who was seated on the Stool of Dignity.

Mawokumiu's civil greeting was ignored as the man launched into a loud tirade about the illegal occupation of a government building, the presence of foreigners in a restricted area, illegal building works and a host of other alleged misdemeanours. The recital seemed endless and the indictments became ever more fanciful until he made the mistake of criticising the behaviour of the villagers in their dealings with the McKenzies.

At this point Mawokumiu interrupted and demanded to see the man's authority and to know the purpose of his visit. Looking suddenly flustered, the man said that he was from the Interior Ministry and that he had come to conduct a census.

The headman again asked to see his authority and the official orders that had brought him there.

"I am here to carry out the official census," he repeated.

The headman again asked to see the documents that gave him authority for this, but the man brushed his request aside. "It is not for an ignorant peasant to question an officer of the national government!" he retorted angrily. "And you should not be harbouring foreigners who have no right to be here, or to occupy an official building. You are hindering the government's business and for this there will be penalties."

The headman reached down and produced a crumpled piece of paper from beneath his stool. "Mr McKenzie tells me this document is a bill of sale from the government, who have sold him the building," he said, smoothing the paper and offering it to the official. "Please read what it says."

"He has no permit to be in this place," the man protested, ignoring the document. "And the government does not sell official buildings, especially not to foreigners."

Mawokumiu offered the document again and asked him once more to read it, but the man brushed it aside, saying it was meaningless rubbish and that the white man had no right to be there.

An idea formed in the headman's mind. He raised his fly whisk and pointed it at the man. "You make claims against this man but offer no reasons to support them. You come here full of your government importance, but bring no evidence of your authority. You insult us by calling us ignorant peasants but, in truth, this is all you are yourself."

With each statement he flicked his fly whisk at the man, "You call McKenzie a foreigner, yet he has government documents permitting him to be here that you have not even seen. This is an important government document," he said, holding up McKenzie's bill of sale, "and yet you ignore it and throw it in the dust without even looking at it."

The government official looked uncomfortable. He had no answers, but soon returned to the attack. "You are an old man, an illiterate peasant, what do you know of government documents?" he shouted. "You have no authority. You are just an old man and simple people grovel because of your age. I am the government officer here. I hold the authority." So saying he pulled a sheaf of papers from his pocket and brandished it in front of Mawokumiu's face. "It is time you and these people learned to be responsible citizens."

With a swiftness that deceived the eye, Mawokumiu reached out and plucked the documents from the man's hand. Ignoring the outraged official, he turned and spoke quietly to one of his sons, who rose and disappeared into a nearby hut. The headman unfolded the papers and inspected each sheet slowly until his son returned, carrying a flat metal box.

Mawokumiu took the heavy necklace of shells and beads from his own neck and passed it through his fingers until he found what he wanted. It was a small key that he then used to unlock the metal box. Lifting the lid, he took out a yellowed roll of paper, tied with a piece of green tape. He called McKenzie to come forward and read out loud what was written on the paper.

It was an official government certificate attesting to Mawokumiu's appointment as Headman and Keeper of the Peace for Asokoné and the surrounding villages. It was dated almost forty years ago and on the back it bore dozens of official stamps that reconfirmed the appointment for every subsequent year.

The villagers received this information with frank amazement and delight. Few, if any of them, appeared to know of this document's existence and none would have been able to read it if they had known. Mawokumiu was their headman because they acknowledged him as such. For most of them he was also their father, so his status was not in dispute. The discovery that he was officially appointed, and had been since long before most of them were born, was a source of great communal pride that only increased his status.

The government man started to protest, but spluttered into silence when Mawokumiu took a pair of steel framed spectacles from his box and perched them on his nose. After a few moments study, he held up the sheaf of papers that he had taken from the government man's hand. "These papers do not give you authority. They are no more than lists of government officers and the places where they are located," the headman said. "Not only that, but they are also out of date."

He lifted the lid of the flat metal box again and brought out a fat brown envelope. The papers inside bore lists similar to those he had taken from the man before him, but the headman's papers were smart and new, not old and much folded. He turned the pages, running his finger down the print until he came to what he sought. "Mawokumiu me'hene Asokoné," he read aloud, "Reconfirmed as Headman and Keeper of the Peace, by His Excellency Ademu Eso Kumubai, Regional Governor, on January 9th, 1971. This is written here. A peasant I may be, but this is my authority and at least I can read it."

There was an awed silence for a moment, followed by loud whoops and cheers. The attentive villagers rose as one, cheering and dancing. The shock discovery that the man whom they all revered for his age and wisdom could also read was cause for yet more celebration.

The official looked horrified. He was obviously out of his depth here and it had never occurred to him that this old man might be able to read. He could barely read himself and was normally only able to identify official documents by their colourful printed headings and the gaudy official stamps they all bore. To add to his embarrassment, he had forgotten to bring his official identity card with him and had no means of proving who he was or why he was here.

Mawokumiu said something to one of his wives, who disappeared inside her hut and returned a few moments later with a covered grass basket. The headman took the basket, piled the official's papers on top and thrust the lot into his hands. "Take yourself back to whatever hole you crawled out of and do not come back," he said. "I do not believe your reason for coming here. There is no need for a census. I know every person here and, as you have seen, I am appointed by the government. If they want to know anything they will write and ask me. You are not an official of our government, just a fool who is rude to honest people." As he spoke he was pushing the man towards the compound gate. "There is food for your journey, which is more than you deserve. Go, and do not come back," he added with finality.

As the headman pushed the man out and slammed the gate behind him, a few of the young men picked up their bows and spears and quietly left by another exit. Mawokumiu ignored them and returned to his stool to talk with the village elders. Nobody saw the officious official's departure, but a few pairs of watchful eyes observed his progress down the mountain. When he stopped at the church and appeared to be about to enter, a shower of small stones clattered on the shiny tin roof and startled him into changing his mind.

Several hours later, two of Mawokumiu's grandsons reported that the man had finally departed and would not be back. By this time, normal life had resumed; women were back tilling their fields and lessons were again in progress at the church.

Some weeks after these events, Mawokumiu walked down to the church to see for himself what the people had achieved. Arriving alone and on foot, he found about twenty of the village boys playing a rather sedate ball game that was in progress on the open ground beside the building, supervised by McKenzie. Mawokumiu sat on a log beneath the only tree nearby that offered some shade and watched.

The boys appeared totally engrossed in their game and soon the headman fell under its spell as he tried to work out the sequence of play. After some minutes, he became aware that he was not alone. Sheila McKenzie was sitting beside him, offering a glass of cool lemonade. Accepting the glass, he asked her what was going on.

"They're playing cricket," replied the missionary's wife. "It is one of our national games and is played in many other countries around the world. It requires patience and discipline as well as great skill and it can also be very tactical." She went on to explain how the game worked and the chief's eyes twinkled bright with delight as he began to understand. At the end of the game, all the boys shook hands and McKenzie came over to talk to his unexpected spectator.

The headman and the missionary sat talking for a long time and darkness was approaching when Mawokumiu finally took his leave. The following afternoon, he again walked down to the church and sat watching as the boys played cricket, observing the careful way in which McKenzie coached them. Afterwards, he and the missionary again sat in discussion until near dark.

Over the next few weeks he went down the hill every few days to watch and to talk. Sometimes a few of his wives accompanied him, but they had little interest in the boys' game and sat happily chatting among themselves in a group a few yards away. Sheila McKenzie soon took advantage of their visits and would sit among them, weaving grass baskets and mats and joining in the chatter.

Many of Mawokumiu's discussions with McKenzie had to do with the church and the doctrine the missionary was preaching. The headman learned fast and soon saw the intricate relationship between his ancient tribal beliefs and this new creed that the McKenzies had woven so skilfully.

As Mrs McKenzie wove mats with the women, she told them tales that bound tradition into the overall pattern of faith and belief. And as her husband built the church, taught lessons or played cricket, he won the hearts and minds of his listeners and tied their own beliefs into this new message. So it was not really surprising when one day the headman told his new young friend – after all, McKenzie was only sixty-seven – that he thought this God of his was a good idea and that he was minded to adopt him.

McKenzie was delighted. He offered to give the headman some formal lessons on doctrine and the practice of his faith before he finally made up his mind and proposed that there should be some sort of confirmation ceremony at which his decision could be publicly declared. Mawokumiu thought this was an excellent idea and suggested that other members of his extended family could also benefit from the teaching. They agreed that McKenzie should visit the headman's compound each day after the evening meal.

And so it was that Mawokumiu sat on the ground every evening, surrounded by a number of his sons, listening to the persuasive teaching of Alec McKenzie. At first, none of his wives attended these lessons, but several listened attentively from behind grass screens and wicker fences, relaying what they had heard to the others later the same night. All that they heard was discussed in infinite detail and compared with the stories that they had heard from Sheila McKenzie as they wove grass mats, sewed or prepared food together. Seldom had Christianity received so much popular attention or such a surge of enthusiasm as it did in Asokoné that summer.

One evening in early December, when McKenzie arrived to give his evening lesson, he found Mawokumiu seated in front of his house on the Stool of Dignity. The elders and many sons were seated with him and a vacant chair awaited McKenzie. He sat down, wondering what matter of great importance had arisen.

He did not have to wait long to find out. As the general hum of conversation subsided, Mawokumiu stood up and announced that he and his sons had been studying hard under the teaching of his good friend McKenzie. They had considered the matter of his God and had decided that He was good. Accordingly, at the time of the next new moon, he and his sons would adopt McKenzie's God. This seemed to him to be an appropriate time as it coincided with the festival McKenzie had told him about when Christians celebrated the birth of God's son Jiziz. This would be the birth of Jiziz in Asokoné.

As the headman sat down, McKenzie, who was not normally given to such sinful emotions as pride, felt a small glow of satisfaction that God's work was indeed being done among these simple folk.

"Your decision is indeed wise," he told the headman. "And you have wise sons too, but there is one small problem that I must bring to your attention."

Mawokumiu looked puzzled, not expecting his acceptance of McKenzie's God to be rejected.

"As Christians," McKenzie continued, "we are allowed to have only one wife, to whom we must remain faithful all our lives. You have had many wives, and still have over eighty living here. How shall we explain this and settle the matter according to God's teaching?"

The headman looked confused. He did indeed have eighty-two wives surviving out of the hundred and sixteen he had married during his long life. He had married each one with all due ceremony, paying the bride price, observing the customary taboos and remaining faithful to every one of them throughout their lives together. How, then, could he only have one wife as a Christian? This was indeed a dilemma.

After a few moments' consideration, Mawokumiu told McKenzie that he would have to think about this problem and discuss the matter with some of his sons, who also had more than one wife each. He withdrew into his house wearing a disappointed air, sad that what should have been a joyful moment had been marred by this unforeseen snag. The listening wives had also appreciated the dilemma, as witnessed by the twitter of female voices that erupted behind the grass screens and fences.

McKenzie stayed for a while and chatted with the villagers before going back down the mountainside and into the church in search of divine guidance for himself. A few minutes later, his wife joined him and they prayed together.

Nothing was seen of Mawokumiu for several days, and the numbers of villagers attending the school began to decline. Those who did come were still friendly, attentive and joined in well, but none said anything about their headman or his dilemma.

A week after the day of his declaration, the headman sent one of his great-grandsons to ask McKenzie to visit him. McKenzie said he would come as soon as the cricket match that was in progress had concluded, and the boy went scampering back up the mountain.

When McKenzie arrived at the headman's compound that evening, he found Mawokumiu seated on a grass mat, surrounded by thirty or so of his sons. The old chief told him that he had been miserable since the last time they had met and this seemed wrong. McKenzie had promised that his God would lead the people into happiness. He still wanted to adopt Him, but needed some advice on how to resolve this dilemma. He could not just abandon most of his wives. Those of his sons who were assembled faced the same problem. He asked McKenzie to tell them all once again about marriage in the Christian tradition.

McKenzie's search for guidance had been long and arduous, but at last he saw a glimmer of opportunity. He preached another of his impromptu sermons on the subject of Christian marriage and then proposed his solution to the particular problem facing Mawokumiu.

"If one of your wives also became a Christian, and you both repeated your vows in a Christian ceremony, then she would be seen as your one wife. The other women could remain in your household and be cared for as they are now without, in the Christian sense, being wives. You would, of course have to refrain from conjugal sports with them," he added, with a meaningful grin.

"It has been some years now since that was possible," said the headman wistfully. "For me it will not be a problem. But as for my sons – they are still vigorous young men."

"Can we not just divorce all the other wives?" asked one of the sons, a man of about McKenzie's age.

McKenzie told him that the promises made on marriage were made for life, and the subject became one of hot debate. Some men wanted to know which wife they should keep. Others maintained that the senior wife of each would have to convert. McKenzie suggested that the women concerned should be consulted. Each one should understand what she was doing if she decided to become a Christian, and none had so far received instruction from McKenzie.

This suggestion was received with horror by some of the men. They were accustomed to their wives doing what they were told, not offering their opinions. That could upset the equilibrium of the whole community.

McKenzie withdrew at this point. "You should talk it out fully and God will guide your thoughts," he said, and went to the church to pray.

The next day, one of the headman's junior wives asked Sheila to visit the women's house and talk with the senior wives. Mawoku-miu had already spoken to them and the most senior had agreed to become a Christian if that was her husband's wish, but first she wanted some advice.

When Sheila McKenzie arrived, she was shown into the women's section of the headman's house and introduced to the senior wife. Emedwe was like a wrinkled little prune, eighty-nine years old, with a cataract in one eye and an ulcerated leg. She had not herself been down to the church, but had heard most of the stories from the other wives, daughters and granddaughters. Now she wished to hear for herself, so that she could decide. Her husband had said she should choose, but not from ignorance.

Although her husband was really the preacher, Sheila McKenzie was as skilful a weaver of words as she was of grass mats, so she settled down to talk as other wives crept in to listen. The women talked all day, but no conclusion was reached.

The following day, when McKenzie saw the headman, Mawokumiu told him that he had asked his senior wife to accept God with him and repeat her marriage vows in the Christian church. McKenzie was delighted. "Unfortunately, there is still a problem," continued the headman. "She has refused. She says that she is too old and worn out for something new like this. She tells me it should be the last wife I married who adopts your God. That one is only forty-six years old and will live to share the end of my life. Emedwe is already old and sick. She expects to join her ancestors soon. I don't know what to do, but I do want to adopt this God."

"Perhaps this is a small test," McKenzie suggested. "God understands what you want to do, but is asking you to resolve this dilemma as a trial of your faith. I have explained how he tests us all, even his own son."

The headman sighed. "I shall talk again to Emedwe," he said.

McKenzie heard nothing for several days – and time was running short. Mawokumiu had insisted that he wanted to become a Christian at Christmas time and that was now only a week away.

On the Sunday before Christmas, the church was full as usual. The congregation was in good voice, but the service ground to a halt when the big doors were pulled open and a group of women entered in the middle of one of the hymns. The party was made up of some of Mawokumiu's junior wives and they were carrying a litter. Emedwe, who could scarcely walk, was propped up on a colourful cushion, dressed in her best clothes. She did not look well.

When McKenzie came forward to welcome her, she seized his hand. "I have come to ask if this Jiziz will accept a sick woman. My man wants to be Christian and is asking me also, so I have come to ask."

"Of course he will accept you," McKenzie replied. "You, and everyone else, will always be welcome in God's family. Let us celebrate this together." The service resumed as the old crone sat in state on her litter and enjoyed the party atmosphere.

Mawokumiu was delighted when he heard what had happened and immediately sent word to McKenzie asking if he could still accept God on Christmas day and whether his marriage would be repeated as part of this ceremony. McKenzie said it could all go ahead as planned and he would be pleased to conduct all the ceremonies together.

Mawokumiu sent one of his sons later that day to ask if the ceremony could include all of his sons who wished to adopt God as well. McKenzie, of course, agreed with a tingle of pleasure.

Two days before Christmas, Emedwe died in her sleep. The headman, who thought his problems were at last resolving themselves, was faced with a new dilemma: would his next wife also accept?

When Emedwe died, the other wives were immediately aware of their husband's dilemma. The next senior wife was hesitant about God and still adhered strongly to the old tribal beliefs. A great discussion began. The young girls who were sent into the women's house to find out what was going on came back with the blunt message that this was women's business and everyone else, including the headman, would have to wait until they had sorted it out.

The argument lasted for a day and a half. Finally, the women emerged. They had resolved the headman's dilemma. One of the younger wives, who had been a frequent participant in the activities at the church, would become a Christian and have her marriage blessed on Christmas day. Later on, the other wives who were keen to adopt the new faith would have a separate ceremony to make them Christians.

McKenzie and Mawokumiu both asked the same question: which of the headman's eighty-one wives had the role of honour? The senior wife answered for them all. Maklinua had been chosen.

"But you are now my senior wife," Mawokumiu protested, still of the opinion that, as the next in line, she herself should have been nominated. "Why not you?"

"Because," she replied firmly, "I am old and no longer good looking. My mind is addled and my eyes do not see well. You need a young wife for this new adventure. One who is lusty and able to learn, one who can accept new ideas with ease and provide the support that the father of Asokoné merits. Maklinua has all these qualities and she is young. She is only seventy years old."

And so it was that on Christmas Day, Mawokumiu and Maklinua duly accepted God and became Christians and the headman's final dilemma was solved.

Anélouha's Secret

As is the case in many rural communities throughout Africa, the inhabitants of Akchinokwe were nearly all related to one another in some way. People had mostly married within the village community and those who had not had usually found spouses in one of the neighbouring villages where, again, just about everybody would be related. Family ties being this close, one might have expected a certain level of inbreeding, with all the problems that this usually brings. Mbaloé was certainly aware of this risk, so he sought a wife from further away.

In 1980, education was still not widespread in his part of the Ivory Coast. Most people had somehow learned to read and write, but only a few had been to school. However, Mbaloé's father had been drafted into the Army during the colonial era and his seven children, although mostly born in the village, had all benefited from his military service by being sent to Army schools. As a result of this superior education, Mbaloé's brothers and sisters had all been able to get jobs in the cities, working in a variety of administrative and commercial roles. They had also found their partners there.

After twenty years in the Army, their father retired with the rank of sergeant and returned to his village to cultivate yams and plantains and to enjoy the status his long service had earned him. Soon afterwards, Mbaloé also returned to the village where he had been born.

On leaving school, he had spent two years at an agricultural college in Ghana. Now he had been appointed as an agricultural development outreach worker for his home area. His job was to introduce new seeds and cultivation techniques, to improve animal husbandry practices, and to encourage people to grow the best foods in support of the nutrition education programmes being conducted by rural health workers.

Mbaloé was welcomed back to the village as a long lost son and he set about reviving the family's farm with enthusiasm. At first, all went well. With his new seeds and tools he made a number of improvements. Under the extended family system, it was his parents, aunts, uncles and cousins who benefited most, since Mbaloé had no wife or children of his own. Even so, tradition is slow to adapt and it was a hard task to persuade people outside his own family to change their ways and adopt new ideas.

He was aware that some of his cousins only tried new things because of his father's influence and it took two full seasons of good results – and free seed from the Agricultural Development Office – to convince them that Mbaloé's new methods and crops had any value.

From the time he had first returned to the village, Mbaloé was very conscious of the fact that he had no wife. A number of families would have welcomed an alliance, but there were few girls of marriageable age in the community. The few there were had either already been promised or had set their sights elsewhere. This posed no problem for Mbaloé, as his work regularly took him to many other villages across the region where there were numerous eligible maidens from whom to choose.

Over a period of several months, he considered various possible candidates in his quest to find the right girl, one who would not only become a good wife, but who would also sustain the status that his position in the community merited. Eventually, his eye settled upon a girl who lived in a village three days walk from his own. He found her very attractive and when she proved responsive to the interest he showed in her, he began the long and convoluted process of formal courtship that was still practised in this region.

Although he was, by any standards, quite a well educated man, his learning had never eroded his appreciation of the traditional values and customs of his people. Mbaloé followed the rituals impeccably, certain that his behaviour would please the spirits of his ancestors and bring blessings, fertility and good fortune to his eventual marriage.

The girl he chose, Anélouha Oyè'ngélé, was also a traditionalist and responded favourably to his advances. Although it would mean moving to a new village three full days' walk from her family home, Anélouha could see potential in this marriage. As the wife of a government official, she would be in a privileged position, her children eligible for the numerous benefits in schooling and health care that were normally accorded to the children of all government employees.

Once married to Mbaloé, her place in society would also be assured. Among these people, authority was vested in the men, but influence, power and prosperity lay firmly within the domain of the women. Anélouha's father was as well pleased with the match as she was when Mbaloé approached him formally to propose marriage.

Returning to his own village, Mbaloé asked one of the elders to serve as his intermediary and the lengthy process of negotiating the bride price then began. It took fourteen weeks for the matter to be settled and a further eight before all the customary exchanges were completed and the wedding could take place.

Mbaloé was not permitted to meet or speak to his intended bride at any time during this period, even though he visited her father frequently. From the day that her father had first agreed to entertain Mbaloé's proposal, Anélouha was secluded among her elder female relatives who instructed and prepared her for marriage.

They fed her on special foods, rubbed her skin with the juices of special plants collected from the forest and tattooed the skin on her shoulders and breasts with traditional designs that embodied her tribal totems and guardian spirits. They instructed her in her matrimonial role and responsibilities and prepared her for the initiation rite that would seal her transformation form adolescence into full womanhood, imbued with the status of her new role. Throughout this time no other man, not even her own father or her brothers, was allowed to see her.

The bride price was paid and tokens and promises were exchanged. A date for the marriage was agreed. At last the appointed day arrived. Accompanied by his own family and many friends from Akchinokwe, Mbaloé went to Anélouha's village to claim his bride.

Still, he was not permitted to see her. There were to be two days of festivities before they would have their first meeting since his proposal had been accepted. This would be at the ceremony when her father would ritually open her to womanhood, using a carved stone phallus. Then, in the presence of both the bride's parents and his own, Mbaloé would be required to consummate the marriage to claim Anélouha as his wife.

As her female relatives brought Anélouha forward, naked and oiled, to be initiated by her father, Mbaloé gasped in shock. Despite her obvious beauty, this was not the slender and attractive girl he had asked to share his life and to become the mother of his children. Although her eyes sparkled in familiar anticipation and her features were similar, this did not look like the same girl at all.

Gone were the long, elegant lines of the slender girl he had met and fallen in love with. Gone was the smooth young face with its ready smile. Gone were the graceful curve of her hips and the smooth flatness of her belly. Gone was the athletic grace of her long limbs and the gentle curve of her neck and shoulders. Gone was the exciting smooth swell of her pert young breasts. This girl was heavy and ponderous. She had pouch cheeks and massive shoulders, with thick limbs, huge heavy breasts, buttocks like a cow buffalo and a large swollen stomach that overhung the dark bush of her sex like the fat round belly of a brewing pot.

Mbaloé knew that it was customary for female relatives to feed a girl up before her wedding, since some of her future status derived from her bulk; but this change was more dramatic than anything Mbaloé could ever have anticipated. If he had not recognised her voice and a particular way in which she used to look at him, he could not have believed it was the same person. Mbaloé's knees felt weak and he wondered how he could have been so terribly deceived. He also felt powerless to do anything.

The village square was crowded with people from Mbaloé's own village as well as his bride's. Drummers filled the air with a deep, throbbing rhythm that was overtly suggestive and enticing. The people around Mbaloé began to sway in time with the drum beat. As Anélouha's father pushed the stone phallus up between her legs, the young men from Mbaloé's village removed his clothing and rubbed his skin with oil and herbs. The witch doctor gave Mbaloé a small gourd filled with a strong smelling infusion. The sorcerer indicated that he should drink it all quickly, as it would make him potent. As if in a trance, Mbaloé complied and the watching women sighed in approval as they watched his manhood rise and he began to move to the rhythm of the drums.

Even as a storm of doubts was raging in Mbaloé's mind, he was swept along in the communal emotion and the inevitable progression of the ritual. As her father withdrew the bloodstained stone from between his daughter's legs, Anélouha reached out and pulled Mbaloé towards her. Her touch hardened his manhood and he moved forward to consummate his marriage, propelled by the impulsive throb of the drums and urged on by the ecstatic sighs of the dried-up old crones who were watching and remembering long ago moments in their own lives when they, too, had experienced the same marriage ritual.

Compelled by the momentum of the event, Mbaloé laid his body on top of his bride. Guided by her firm hands, he entered and thrust. As he did so he felt something jab softly upwards from her belly into his own. He withdrew and thrust again. Again he was prodded firmly in the belly and his mind went into a spinning turmoil. Without understanding what it could possibly be, he was acutely aware that something was not as it should be. His manhood shrivelled and he fell back, rolling off the girl and subsiding into a shaking heap on the ground.

The watching parents observed the couple's bloodied genitals and knew that Mbaloé had entered. The marriage had been consummated and was valid. Mbaloé and Anélouha were now man and wife. In the morning they would return to Akchinokwe for three more days of feasting before settling down to married life together.

Young men crowded round and lifted Mbaloé to their shoulders. The young women lifted Anélouha and the surging mass of singing, gyrating people carried the newlyweds round the village to proclaim their union to the whole community and to the ancestral spirits. At significant points on their route they paused to give the couple ritual foods and drink before they were carried onwards by the exuberant crowd.

At dawn the festivities returned to the village meeting place and Anélouha's father gave Mbaloé a gourd of maize beer. By drinking this, Mbaloé irrevocably accepted full responsibility for his new bride. As he took the gourd from Anélouha's father, doubts again filled Mbaloé's mind. Whilst he could not identify the exact nature or cause of his unease, he felt instinctively that something was amiss, but, unable to give form to his doubts, he had no option but to accept his new responsibility. This was to be the final confirmation of their union. Any faltering or refusal now would condemn them both to a life of ignominy and derision throughout the region.

The crowd fell silent as he raised the gourd to his lips. He paused, looking round as if seeking the reason for his anxiety. The air became electric with tense anticipation. The waiting crowd fell silent. The drumbeat faded to silence. Mbaloé looked at his bride, saw again the twinkle in her eyes and the slight tilt of the head that had first brought her to his attention, and felt again the thrill of their first encounter, their first embrace.

He drank the beer in one long draught. As he swallowed, a collective sigh of satisfaction escaped from several hundred mouths as the onlookers released their bated breath.

The festivities in Mbaloé's own village were joyful and prolonged. This was a high status marriage and merited elaborate celebration lasting a full three days. During all that time, although Mbaloé and Anélouha were constantly together, they had not a single moment alone. It was not until the fourth day that they were able to withdraw into their own hut and close the door. Only then could Mbaloé talk to his bride and discover exactly what the old women of her father's family had done to produce such a startling change in her appearance.

Although shocked by this transformation, Mbaloé was soon reassured that it was only her shape that had altered. He found that her bubbly nature was still intact and her affection and desire to please him was as strong as ever. Her enthusiasm for life and her lively intelligence were unaltered. She was still the girl he had fallen in love with. He also discovered that she was pregnant.

This came as something of a shock to Mbaloé. It was customary for a girl to be a virgin when she married, the opening ritual carried out by the father giving public testimony to his daughter's purity. It was certainly almost unheard of for a girl to be with child at the time of her marriage.

Mbaloé was both horrified and fascinated by this stupendous news. He readily accepted his bride's assurances that the child could only be his, well remembering the glorious afternoon they had spent in the long grass by the river when Anélouha had agreed to become his wife. He was sure that from that moment on she had been his alone and that she would not have given so much as a thought to another man. And yet he was stunned that a single afternoon's intimacy could have produced such a momentous result.

Because of her premarital seclusion, Anélouha had been unable to tell Mbaloé – and it was certainly not the sort of message a girl could send to her betrothed by means of messenger, however well trusted. She had realised very early on what had happened, but had no means of sharing the news. She was both excited at the prospect of becoming the mother of Mbaloé's child and apprehensive lest he reject her at the wedding for being impure.

Anélouha had not spoken of her condition to any of the other women as they prepared her for marriage, for much was being made of her virginity. The old women had told lurid tales of their own initiations and their first sexual experiences that were far removed from what Anélouha and Mbaloé had shared that afternoon by the river. They devoted endless hours of discussion to the status she would have as such a beautiful and pure bride. They were all impressed by her appetite, so she had simply eaten as much as she could of all the special foods they provided in the hope that her increased weight would disguise her condition and distract any observant eyes from speculation.

Happily, there had been little foetal movement and the first time her unborn child had really moved was when her father thrust the ritual stone penis between her legs at her initiation. Its shaft was slightly roughened to ensure that she bled and she was sure, until the moment when Mbaloé withdrew so suddenly, that nobody else had detected her secret. Even he seemed uncertain, and she was very relieved to see that he did not reject her. Her doubts persisted, however, until he had swallowed her father's gourd of maize beer.

In the quiet intimacy of the marital home, Mbaloé's doubts soon subsided. He realised that some public explanations might be necessary, but there was time enough for those later. Anélouha reassured him that she had been his alone since that afternoon down by the river and that no man had touched her before that time. Mbaloé was content with this and said that he had felt the same. "So I did marry a virgin," he told his wife. "Even if she was a pregnant virgin!"

"There is more," Anélouha told her husband shyly. "You are very potent, for I am carrying twins."

"Then I have married a doubly pregnant virgin!" laughed Mbaloé with delight.

Hippopotamus Hiatus

The gallery forest came right down to the river banks, opposing green walls two hundred feet high, with a narrow gap of maybe a hundred and fifty feet from bank to bank through which the river flowed. Over time, the river had carved its channel downwards and the banks now stood thirty-five feet above the normal water level, with small clefts and scars where smaller streams joined the flow and where people had cut pathways down to the water. On the inside of some of the bends there were small shingle beaches where women would congregate to wash clothing or children would come to play and swim. One such beach existed just below my house, at the bottom end of our village, and the well-worn zigzag path down to it started a few yards from my house. When I had first come to live in the village, I had tied a long rope to the overhanging branch of a tall flame tree and secured an old rubber tyre to the end of it. This now hung a few feet above the water, some ten feet out from the bank, and had become a very popular swing for the twenty-nine children of the village.

The forest is seldom silent and, except for a short period in the early afternoon when most of the animal and avian population takes a short siesta, there is normally a symphony of bird calls, insect noises and howls from passing primates to fill one's ears. Below the village, the air was also alive for much of the time, with the merry shrieks of children swinging out on the rope to splash into the water.

Whilst most of the villagers could swim and everyone used the river for some purposes, the villagers were essentially forest folk, not riverine, and they had neither boats nor canoes of their own. Although our villagers caught a few fish with spears or hook and line, fishing was generally left to specialists from other villages who came down in their canoes to trade fish for forest fruits, nuts and yams every week.

Although there were some quite large fish, we got very few crocodiles in our bit of river. This was partly because crocodiles were not very common in the region, but also because a small herd of hippopotamus had taken up residence on an island about a mile downstream. As a rule, they didn't venture up as far as the village, but their very presence in the river was a deterrent to crocodiles. So the villagers left the hippos in peace and they, in turn, left us alone.

As a result, it was comparatively safe to swim from the beach below the village, except when the river was in flood. The water was clear, slow flowing and normally too shallow for anything as large as a hippopotamus to approach submerged. Even so, the children, who were wise to the ways of their environment, usually positioned one of their number high in the tree to act as a lookout. The sentry seldom had to warn of danger, but was usually the first to announce the approach of a trading canoe with fish from one of the villages upstream. There was rarely any other traffic on the river. It was too shallow for timber barges, so there was no logging in the area, and we were beyond the range of the government patrols that regularly cruised the main rivers of the Congo basin.

When I had first come to live in the area, I had taken over an abandoned house at the bottom end of the village and had rebuilt it. The walls had been sound and only needed a little repair with clay from the river bank. The roof had to be entirely replaced, with new rafters made from straight forest saplings bound together with vines cut from the undergrowth just a few yards from my front door. On top of the rafters were thick mats woven from palm leaves and tied down with raffia bindings. The whole structure was then covered in a thick layer of thatch made from a different species of palm leaf that stayed waxy and waterproof for a long time. The villagers, of course, knew which were the best plants for every purpose and seemed more than happy to help and to teach me.

Although the people in this part of the forest tended some plants, they didn't really do much cultivation. Their version of agriculture was more a matter of harvesting what the forest offered and taking care of special plants that they discovered during their forest forays. The idea of clearing ground and planting a crop, whilst not unknown, was nevertheless alien to their culture. My decision to clear a plot of jungle near my house for cultivation was therefore the subject of much speculative discussion and more than a few jokes at my expense. The fact that the crop I proposed to plant was bananas was greeted with frank disbelief. The forest was full of bananas. Any of the village children could have found me a whole treeful of ripe fruits within a few minutes. Why should I plant something that was already abundant?

The answer was simple. During my own wanderings in the forest I had discovered a stand of rather unusual banana trees. The skin of the fruit was deep pink in colour rather than yellow, while the flesh was creamy and exquisitely tasty. The smell, too, was deliciously sweet and un-banana like. Most of the fruit had already been eaten by other forest dwellers before I came across the isolated stand of trees, but what little remained was enough to make me realise, when I sampled them, that these bananas were special.

When I asked about them in the village I was told that they were indeed prized as the tastiest of all bananas, but that they were rare and very hard to find. It was then that I conceived the idea of transplanting some of the suckers and trying to grow a few trees nearer to the village.

Given that the fruit was considered such a delicacy, I was a little surprised that our villagers seemed unaware of this particular clump of trees. The reason became clear when I was talking to the Akuamba Kau, our itinerant witch doctor, who explained to me that they were in an area of the forest where people did not go because they believed it to be the home of a malevolent spirit. I asked if this meant that I should not touch the banana suckers in case they brought the spirit with them to the village and he laughed. He said he would come with me when I went to collect the suckers and seek permission of the spirits for me to remove them. He, too, was partial to red bananas and regretted the fact that the birds and monkeys invariably got there first. Maybe if I were to grow some, he might have a few? He knew, of course, that I would deny him nothing.

And so it was that I cleared my plot, about the size of a tennis court, and prepared the ground for planting. This took some time because, apart from the thick tangle of undergrowth, there were a lot of saplings and two substantial trees that had to be removed. One of the trees was ideal for the ridge of the new village meeting house that had long been proposed but never built. The saplings and a few smaller trees would provide most of the other material for the building's framework and rafters, while the vines and bark would serve as string to bind this all together. I received help with the clearance work from a couple of the men and not long after that job had been completed, we were able to set about building the new meeting house in the centre of the village.

When I had finished preparing the ground, I approached the Akuamba Kau and asked him for his assistance in collecting the suckers for my new banana patch. We agreed to meet in the forest near the place where I had found the trees. He would then approach the spirits and ask their permission for me to dig up the things I needed.

The Akuamba Kau was already there when I arrived, a little late. Whenever I set off into the forest, someone in the community always insisted on keeping me company. This was partly because they were very sociable people, who never do anything entirely alone, and partly because everyone knew I was keen to learn about the forest and they all loved to show me things. There was also the fact that they were all intensely nosey and always wanted to know what I was doing. As a result, it had taken me longer than usual to get clear of the village without being accompanied. It was only when I told Ekwona, the village headman, that I was going to seek the advice of the Akuamba Kau that he instructed his people to let me go alone, for it was accepted that nobody should intrude on such consultations uninvited.

The Akuamba Kau's reputation is such that he is viewed with great respect and admiration, verging on reverence yet tinged with a slight wariness because he is *niseki*. This is a term used to cover a whole range of complex ideas and beliefs relating to those who have contact with the spirit world or who demonstrate abilities and qualities beyond the normal comprehension of ordinary people. Whilst it is normally used in a positive sense, there are also circumstances in which it can convey overtones of suspicion or apprehension. Thus it was accepted that since I wanted to consult a man who was the embodiment of all these qualities, I should be left alone to do so. It was also accepted that I needed no company, since I would be under the Akuamba Kau's protection.

His ritual to obtain the spirits' consent took little time and he was delighted to find a few ripe fruits in the grove when we approached. He saw this as a good omen and settled down to eat some fruit whilst I dug up the suckers I needed and stacked them in my basket. In between mouthfuls, he told me many interesting things about the lore of the forest, the plants that grew there and the ways of its people. In the months since I had come to live and work in the forest, this extraordinary man had been a wonderful teacher and had become a very good friend. He was also, as I had discovered, the grandfather of Abélé, a village girl whose parents had died and whom I had been persuaded to foster. As a result, he often came and ate at our hearth – although he never slept in the village. Nobody actually knew where he lived, but he had an uncanny knack of always turning up when needed or at the time of momentous events, only to depart again as mysteriously as he had arrived, melting away unnoticed and with no word of farewell.

It took me an hour of hard work to dig up enough banana suckers to fill my basket. After that, there was a three-hour walk back to the village. Travel anywhere in a tropical rainforest is slow and the vines and undergrowth grow so fast that within as little as a few hours a freshly cut path will become partly obscured. It had taken me some months to learn how to move through the forest without having to hack my way through step-by-step. Now, I seldom had to wield my machete, although I always carried it with me, but, even so, the heavy basket made travel somewhat slower than usual as it kept snagging on things. We were also delayed by the need to take shelter for a couple of hours during the intense downpour that occurred regularly every evening at about seven o'clock. We finally arrived back in the village long after dark, when most of the villagers had already settled for the night. Abélé had food waiting for us and after we had eaten the old man got up and vanished silently into the forest.

As I dug the first hole to plant a sucker the following morning, I was aware of somebody watching me from the bushes. I thought it would be one of the villagers, but it was the old witch doctor. He had returned to give his blessing to my endeavour and to ask the spirits to make my planting successful. I nodded a greeting and carried on planting, spacing out the forty-six suckers so as to cover the whole plot. Later, when I next went up to Kikwit, I would obtain some vegetable seeds from the Chinese research station near the town. I wanted to plant peppers and tomatoes between the bananas. Until they grew up and their foliage started to spread, there should be enough light for a few vegetables to grow underneath. Whether or not they flourished as well as I hoped, it would be fun to try.

Leaving Abélé to look after the house and tend my young banana plants, I was away from the village for most of the next couple of weeks. A village five days' walk away to the north of us had sought my help in sorting out a polluted spring that had been their principal source of drinking water. When I returned, the plants were already above waist height and all of them had survived. I spent an afternoon planting tomato and pepper seeds between the bananas and then turned my attention to work on the new meeting house that was beginning to take shape in the centre of the village.

Downstream from our village, on the far bank of the river, someone had cleared an area of forest and planted coffee trees. Whilst these were not unknown in the forest, this seemed an odd thing to have done since it was generally too hot and humid for coffee to thrive. Nevertheless, the owner had planted some small bushes and they were growing reasonably well, although it required a great deal of labour to keep the ground free of weeds and to stop the jungle regenerating itself on the cleared ground. I wondered why he hadn't planted oil palms, since there was an oil mill a couple of miles further down the river that depended almost entirely on palm fruits from wild palms scattered through the forest. To have a plantation nearby could have been very worthwhile, but the owner was determined to have coffee. His plantation was just round the bend, upstream of the island where the hippopotamus herd had taken up residence. The hippos seldom ventured far from their island, which was covered in lush vegetation, remaining quite content to graze the grassy flats just downstream, where they were able to harvest the many hundreds of tons of weeds, water hyacinths and other vegetation that came floating down on the gentle current in a never ending stream of fresh greenery.

Everything grows very quickly in the steamy heat of the jungle. My vegetables germinated within a few days and before long the plants were a foot tall. The banana suckers, too, grew apace and soon opened their huge leaves to form floppy umbrellas. These were torn, as so often happens with banana leaves, by the tremendous weight of water that fell during the regular early evening downpours, but still the plants grew. In less than three months the first flower spikes appeared and were immediately surrounded by clouds of furiously buzzing insects and delicate nectar-loving sun birds that came to feed off the flowers. Soon afterwards, the first fruits appeared; stubby little upward pointing fingers in groups of five that ringed the extending flower spike from the bottom upwards. Unlike the cultivated bananas usually found in European supermarkets, which grow in upward-facing hands on hanging stems, these forest varieties grow on a stalk that pushes straight up from the centre of the plant to a height of about six feet. The fruit therefore stands above the leaves, which is important if they are to ripen, for they must get as much as possible of the light that filters through the dense canopy a hundred and fifty feet or more overhead. Even though my banana plot had originally been open to the sky, it had only taken a few weeks for the surrounding trees to extend their canopies sideways and the direct sun was already noticeably reduced. However, because I had cleared the ground and maintained the plantation, the suckers I had planted had taken advantage of not having to compete with dense undergrowth and had fruited early without wasting effort trying to push their flower spikes above the competition.

The villagers' scepticism and jokes at my idea of planting

bananas had by now given way to great interest and anticipation, for undoubtedly they would all get a share of any fruit that the plants managed to produce. They were already happily munching my tomatoes and peppers. And although nobody else had yet started to cultivate anything, their interest had certainly been roused and I had real hopes that some of them might try growing something themselves once the construction of the new meeting house, which had been taking up all their spare time, was completed. I had learned that they had to feel the need before embarking on any new project, otherwise it was doomed. That had been the case with constructing a filter on the village spring, and again with the new meeting house. Only when opportunity and need created the imperative did work begin. Once my crop had all been eaten up they might perhaps make some effort to grow their own, I thought.

To my great surprise and delight it happened sooner than that. Tslege, one of the older men in the village, had taken a great deal of interest when I was planting the banana suckers and had sat on a nearby log, watching intently as I worked. He asked a lot of questions and seemed genuinely interested, but he never lifted a finger to help me. This didn't surprise me as he had a reputation for being lazy and his wife was constantly nagging him. He watched again when I planted the tomatoes and peppers and even asked me why I didn't bring plants from the forest for this, too. It was only when he saw my plants bear fruit that he began to understand, but then he wanted to know why these varieties didn't grow wild in the forest? My explanation did nothing to satisfy his curiosity, so one day when I was going up to Kikwit I asked him to come with me and we went on to visit the Chinese agricultural research station ten miles the other side of the town. His eyes opened wide with amazement at the abundance of crops and his delight grew all the more when the Chinese technicians gave us a parting gift of a basket of assorted vegetables. Unbeknown to me, one of them also gave Tslege a small packet of seeds, which he stuffed in his pocket and said nothing about.

Three days later I noticed that some of the tools that usually leaned against the side wall of my house had gone. It was common for people to borrow items like this and, since they always brought them back, I thought no more about it. Sure enough, a couple of days later the tools reappeared. It must have been another week before I had cause to go up to the top end of the village, which was where Tslege lived. When I did, I was surprised to discover a patch of ground about five yards square that had been cleared, neatly dug and planted with rows of three distinct sorts of little plants. There were tomatoes, sweet potatoes and something I had not seen before, which turned out to be a form of squash.

To protect his crop, Tslege had built a low fence of palm matting propped up on toasted sticks. This amused me. He evidently wanted to make sure that his fence posts didn't grow. Any bit of freshly cut stick was liable to sprout and grow if it was pushed into the ground here. To prevent this happening with the saplings we had used as upright poles for the new meeting house, we had stripped them of their bark and toasted them over a low fire for a day or more before putting them in position.

I knew Tslege had spotted me looking at his work, although he kept away from me for a few more days. When I did eventually bump into him, I told him what a fine job he had done and admired the health of his plants. He shrugged off my compliments, but I could see that he was pleased with my reaction. I hoped other people in the village would share my feelings about his effort and decide to copy them and so resolved to have a word with the witch doctor. Maybe if he commented favourably others would feel more inclined to make the effort too.

As things turned out, we did not see the Akuamba Kau in the village for another three and a half weeks and by the time he did come, other events had completely driven these thoughts from my mind.

Late one evening, we heard a lot of noise coming from somewhere downriver from the village. Sound travels quite some distance in the forest, especially after the heavy early evening rain has cleared the air. Some sounds travel better than others and this is particularly true of gunshots. The noise that had first attracted our attention had been going about five minutes before we heard a series of single shots, not quite evenly spaced, and a great deal of loud roaring and screaming. One of the villagers thought that hunters from another village must have caught a forest elephant and were trying to kill it. Nothing else could make noises like that, he maintained, unless there was a new evil spirit loose in the forest that was screaming its rage because somebody had upset it.

The following morning, we found out exactly what all the noise had been about. Mputu brought the news. He was a young lad from our village who worked as a mechanic at the palm oil mill a few miles downstream. Every week, he came home for a couple of days to see his family. He was also more than a little sweet on Abélé. He used to tinker with my old Landrover as an excuse to be near her and never missed an opportunity to come home.

The previous evening's noises had been caused by a pair of hippos that had left the island and ventured a little further than usual from their home territory. They had come ashore on the far bank some time during the heaviest rain and had started munching their way through the farmer's coffee plantation.

By the time someone discovered what was happening, it was almost too late. They had eaten most of the young bushes and were guzzling at the fresh forest sprouts that were emerging round the edges of the plantation. The farmer's family and friends had made as much noise as possible, in an effort to scare them off, while one of his sons rushed down to the palm oil mill to see if the manager would come with his gun. It was he who had fired the shots, Mputu told us, and his description had everyone in stitches as he re-enacted the manager's attempts to load and fire his rusty old single barrelled shotgun.

Mputu had brought a couple of jugs of palm wine back with him and these were passed around while he was telling the story. As a result, something of a party atmosphere soon developed in the village as his tale continued to unfold. I had a few bottles of beer in my house and some of the village wives had been fermenting forest fruits, so a variety of different concoctions added to the jollity.

When the hippos finally returned to the river, Mputu told us, there were less than a hundred coffee bushes still intact out of the eight thousand the farmer had planted. Those that had not been eaten had been trampled into the mud that had been churned up by the panicking hippos when the people tried to drive them off. By morning, the hippos had returned to their island and quiet had been restored.

The oil mill manager was apparently now trying to persuade the farmer to plant oil palms, since hippos never ate these, presumably because the spiky fronds were leathery and unpalatable, with little food value. The only problem was that it would take at least five years for the palms to get big enough to start producing fruit and a further three before these gave any appreciable quantity of oil. I expected Tslege, who was normally the village cynic, to say it was because the farmer had been interfering with the forest that this had happened, but since he too was now a cultivator, albeit in a very small way, he wisely kept his counsel.

The following night I was woken at three o'clock by Abélé shaking me and telling me there were monsters outside. I went to the door and heard some heavy low rumbling sounds and a few grunts. There was also the sound of something large moving about in the forest. I sent Abélé to rouse Ekwona, the headman, and some of the other villagers. I, meanwhile, sought out the pile of stout stakes that I had stacked beside the house. I bound rags round one end of each of them and dipped them into the sump oil that Mputu had collected when he changed the oil in my Landrover that afternoon. Then, once a number of village men had gathered, we lit them from the embers of my cooking fire.

With blazing torches held aloft, a line of us moved cautiously towards the source of the strange noises that were coming from somewhere between my house and the river bank. We only had to go a few yards to discover what it was. A large hippopotamus was standing in the centre of my banana patch, placidly munching its way through my precious plants. As we approached, it turned and looked at us, its large eyes glowing red in the flickering light from the flames, and calmly continued munching.

Apart from the burning torches, none of us had a weapon of any sort, but we were probably better off without. The last thing we needed was an enraged, injured hippo marauding through the village, for these are highly dangerous animals at the best of times, responsible for more deaths than crocs, big cats or any other of the more recognised killers.

There was a hasty whispered discussion about what to do and, finally, we decided to try and guide the beast back towards the river by waving our flaming torches at it. One of the young boys, who had woken and joined the men, was sent back into the village with instructions to prepare more torches and bring more people. Within minutes, he returned with half a dozen more people and others following behind and the number of torches soon grew until we could present a wall of fire to the hippo.

The uninvited guest, meanwhile, was calmly continuing his meal. As our number grew, some of the men started making buzzing noises and waving their torches up and down in front of them. Soon, everyone followed suit and the dancing wall of fire gradually started to surround the hippo, until only the path towards the river was left open. Ekwona, who always lead the hunt in the forest, made some different clicking noises and slowly the line of torch bearers began to move forward. At some point, the hippo decided it didn't like being surrounded by fire and turned towards the gap. As he passed through, heading down the path to the river, one of the men ran forward and pushed his burning torch hard into the retiring rump. With a squeal, the hippo charged forward and soon disappeared from view. Several of the men nearest followed it down the path, shouting now to reinforce their torches. Moments later we heard a large splash and knew that it had reached the river. The men who had followed it down the path told us that they had managed to inflict at least two large burns on the hippo's rump, so that if it came again we would be able to recognise it. Meanwhile, not surprisingly, it had departed in great haste.

The torches were burning low by this time and it was impossible to see any detail in the banana patch. We retired to the clear area in front of my house to sit and talk about the night's events. Since most of the village's current production of fermented brews had been consumed the previous night when Mputu brought us news about the coffee plantation, we had to make do with tea or fresh fruit for refreshment. This scarcely mattered and, with dawn approaching, nobody felt the least like sleeping.

When daylight came, so did our mysterious witch doctor. The Akuamba Kau was standing at the edge of the plot, in the same spot as he had occupied the day I had planted the banana suckers, surveying the devastation. Almost everything had been eaten. It was as though I had just cleared the ground ready for planting. Only two banana trees remained and both bore heavy stalks of ripening fruit. I went over, collected the ripest and then invited the Akuamba Kau to come and eat with me. As we sat down, Abélé brought tea. A few moments later Tslege appeared with a basket of ripe tomatoes.

"You have paid your debt to the spirit for taking the banana trees," he said, thrusting the tomatoes into my hands. "Now I wish to pay what I owe you for teaching me to grow food."

"You had no debt, but if you had it was paid the day you planted your seeds," I told him and handed him some ripe red bananas in return.

"Will you try again?" asked the Akuamba Kau, a trifle wistfully, as he bit into a banana.

"The planting is already done," I said. "The trees that were eaten have already produced suckers that are below the ground. In a few days they will emerge and within a week they will be as high as my knees."

A week later, the three of us stood again beside my banana plot, admiring the thirty-two new plants that were indeed almost knee high.

Immigration Control

After five weeks leave in Britain, I went to Accra for a week to attend the African Population Conference. I was to go on from there to Lomé in Togo, which is all of sixty-five miles along the coast. There was no coach service in those days and, unless one had access to a car, road travel depended on bush taxis or mammy wagons. The only other alternative was to fly on the twice weekly service provided by Air Afrique, which took the form of an antiquated Dakota. I would have been happy to go by bush taxi, crammed into an overcrowded car with at least eight other adults and a huge pile of luggage strapped to the roof, but my masters insisted that I went by air.

Inevitably, the flight was delayed by a technical problem and the sun was high and the air already baking hot by the time we eventually walked across the apron to the waiting aircraft at Accra airport. There had already been some good entertainment in the terminal, resulting from the Air Afrique staff's solemn insistence on weighing every item of baggage very carefully and then refusing to allow a single pound of overweight luggage go on board, regardless of one's willingness to pay. The flight was full, they said, and the weight factor was critical. One very large American lady, who was predisposed to whine about everything, made a tremendous fuss about having to discard thirty pounds of items from her matching luggage.

The rest of us simply opened our cases, removed dispensable items such as toiletries that could be replaced easily and repacked our bags. Having done this, however, I found that my bag was still about four pounds overweight. There was only one thing for it. I took my bag to the gents and repacked it. In went the lightweight tropical suit I had been wearing and I emerged a few minutes later wearing my heavy kilt with all the accoutrements and my bag weighing less than the required limit. The people waiting for flights that day were a colourful lot and nobody took any notice or saw anything out of place about my attire.

The bags were checked and taken out to be loaded into the plane's hold. Eventually the passengers were summoned to board and a long crocodile of droopy people straggled across the roasting apron towards a line of waiting planes. As it became clear which plane we were to board, the whining American started again.

"Ah dun payed fer a prapper airplane ride, not a trip in some anti deeloovian death trap like that tin can! I wanna proper plane!" she wailed as her husband tried to look as though she was nothing to do with him.

The pilot, a phlegmatic Frenchman with a world weary face, was waiting at the foot of the boarding ladder. As the woman hung back and repeated her protest he turned and shrugged.

"Madame, in two minutes I shall close the door," he announced "Then I will start les moteurs and we shall depart. If you are not on board, I shall leave you be'ind." With this he skipped up the rickety ladder and disappeared inside the aircraft. The American woman, whose husband had already boarded, hurried after him and the door slammed closed behind her.

It was not worth climbing to any altitude for a twenty-five-minute flight, so the pilot stayed low and we were treated to a grandstand view of the coastal plain from just over two thousand feet. We had the coast on one side and lush palm groves and fields of corn and cassava stretching away northwards to the forest on the other. In the hot tropical air, turbulence was already building up and so the pilot left the 'Fasten Seat Belts' sign illuminated. The only other member of the crew, a pretty African stewardess, handed out sweets and cool moist face cloths for our comfort. The only unpleasant part of the flight was the incessant whining of the fat American woman. We had not been airborne more than ten minutes before the pilot engaged his autopilot, left his seat and came back into the cabin to ask her to be quiet.

Hijackings were unheard of in those days and there was no door between the cabin and the flight deck. We could all see that there was no co-pilot, so when the pilot came back and spoke to the American woman there was nobody up front. When he had said his piece and calm was momentarily restored, the woman unfortunately made this same observation.

"Hey! Who's flying this darn crate with you standin here?" she demanded.

"Nobody, madame," the pilot replied. "There was too much distraction from you and I could not even 'ear my radio. If you do not shut up, I will not go back. Then we will crash in the sea and the sharks can get fat eating you!" He turned to the other passengers with a gallic shrug.

The woman immediately started another wailing protest, which stopped abruptly a moment later as her husband's fist landed heavily on the point of her jaw. As she sagged unconscious in her seat he looked up and said calmly: "Sorry about that, Captain. She'll be quiet now."

The pilot gave another shrug and returned to his seat. Soon afterwards we flew over the city of Lomé and landed at the new airport. The terminal building was airy and cool after the stuffy confines of the plane's crowded cabin. Lines of whirring fans hung above our heads and blew a gentle breeze over us as we queued to have our passports checked. When my turn came, the Immigration Officer's eyes flicked briefly over me before he examined my passport. He looked at the photograph, which had been taken at a time when my beard was much shorter, and checked it against my face. Then he looked down at my feet and his eyes travelled slowly upwards until he again reached my face. Holding up my passport and waving it in the air, he spoke to one of his colleagues, who also came over to inspect me. After studying the passport photo, he, too, inspected me from shoes to face.

"Mais c'est fantastique!" he declared, staring at my kilt. "C'est Monsieur ou Mademoiselle?"

Needless to say, everyone except the Americans, who spoke no French, thought this was outrageously funny and the whole terminal joined in the laughter. When I presented my bag at the customs bench the joke was repeated and we all laughed some more as the officers scribbled their chalk marks on every bag that was presented without so much as a question about the contents. Goodness knows what contraband came through undetected that morning, but nobody's baggage got opened, not even the Americans'.

I don't know how many times my hand was shaken that morning, but I believe I must have been greeted by every official in the place and I was very tempted to get my bagpipes out and play them. I eventually made it to the exit door, where I found someone waiting to meet me. I tossed my baggage into the back of the dusty Landrover and we headed into the city in the direction of a cold beer and lunch.

Six weeks later, I had cause to fly from Lomé up to Niamey, in Niger. The local travel agent provided a ticket and advised me to be at the check-in desk at least half an hour before the departure time. The security checks that we are so familiar with today were not even thought of at that time and check-in was certain to be brief since I would be returning within two days and was only taking a small bag. I arrived at the check-in with a little time to spare and presented my ticket. A boarding pass was issued and I headed towards passport control and the departure lounge.

As I presented my passport, I immediately recognised the Immigration Officer. He was the same man I had met when I arrived. He looked at my passport, inspected me from head to toe and shook his head.

"Ça ne va pas," he announced. "Vous êtes arrivé en Mademoiselle, vous ne pouvez pas partir en Monsieur."

"What do you mean?" I asked

"The kilt," he replied, grinning. "You must wear it to pass control."

"But it is back at my house," I protested. "I will miss the flight."

"The plane will wait," he assured me. "You must wear it."

"Really? Is it necessary? I'll have to go all the way home to change," I told him.

"Oui. C'est necessaire," he insisted.

There was nothing for it but to go home and change. I arrived back in a taxi with the wheels squealing round the corners, but needn't have worried about rushing. As promised, the flight had been held up for almost an hour. The passengers had been served iced drinks and word had obviously gone round about the reason for the delay. I was given a rousing cheer when I finally climbed the steps and took my seat.

I made eleven more flights in or out of Lomé airport over the next eighteen months and every time it was the same: I was required to wear my kilt. After the first couple of flights, by which time I had learned to make sure that I turned up 'properly dressed', I no longer even needed to show my passport. I soon got to know all the airport officials and found, in those eighteen months, that I had made some very good friends.

A Girl Named Ian

In the early 1970's, what was then called Upper Volta and is now known as Burkina Faso was the poorest country in the world. The economy, such as it was, was entirely underpinned by the French and the annual budget was less than France's defence expenditure for a week. The country's location on the southern fringe of the Sahara meant that agriculture was barely at subsistence level; infant mortality was over thirty-five per cent and for most people life expectancy was less than forty years. Only a fraction of the total population of three and a half million lived in the two principal cities – Ouagdougou, the centrally situated capital, and Bobo-Dioulasso in the more fertile south western corner of the country – and yet the only two hospitals were situated in these two cities, the rest of the country depending on small clinics in provincial villages. These clinics were often run by Christian missionaries of various denominations. Few of them had doctors, and most were staffed by one or more foreign missionary nurses, with sometimes a locally recruited and partially trained nurse or midwife to help them out.

Missionaries and their stations fell into two groups: the older Catholic missions, that were established during the colonial era and whose nuns and priests had spent a lifetime of service in the country, and the more recently installed Protestant missions, most of which were less than fifteen years old and had their origins in North America. The Catholics lived at a gentle pace, in tune with the local culture. They provided pastoral care that was designed to fit in with way the people led their lives – ministering to the sick without question, running small schools and inviting everyone to join in with their religious services, ceremonies and festivals without putting any real pressure on them to do so.

The Protestants were altogether more aggressively evangelical.

They doled out pills for the sick and sermons for all those who came seeking treatment. Any pastoral care that was offered was invariably conditional on the recipients sitting through a vigorous religious lecture that was as critical of their traditional life and beliefs as is it was promotional of the mission's evangelical ideals.

The mission station at Piéla was one such mission and I had been asked by a British development charity organisation to visit and evaluate their request for financial help to build a new dispensary and maternity unit. As this was the only health provision within a radius of about fifty miles and as it boasted two trained expatriate nursing staff, it appeared to be a worthwhile project and a quick response would be helpful. The only difficulty was that Piéla is situated about a hundred and ten miles north east of Ouagadougou, in an area where roads are few and very poorly maintained and as it was now the rainy season, such roads as did exist were likely to be impassable, even with a four-wheel-drive vehicle. The missionaries, whose only ground transport was said to be a Mobylette scooter and a donkey cart, were normally able to overcome this problem thanks to the small airstrip that had been cleared and which enabled them to maintain contact with the outside world through periodic visits of their Society's own aircraft.

Unfortunately, this had been grounded for a major overhaul and, as a result, it seemed unlikely that anyone from the NGO would be able to visit for at least five months. So, since I was working in the region on a series of government sponsored development projects and had an aircraft at my disposal, I was asked to make the visit and evaluate the project.

When I called up on the radio to let the mission know that I would be visiting, I asked the missionary, a Canadian called Peterson, to confirm the mission's exact geographical location, but when he heard that I intended to fly in he seemed more than a little sceptical about whether I would ever be able to find the place. I told him not to worry and that, thunder storms permitting, I would be there at half-past three the following afternoon. I added that if they were short of any light supplies, I would be only too happy to bring them with me from the capital, but he assured me they had everything they needed. Even so, I bought a couple of bottles of drinkable French wine to take with me.

The following morning, I prepared my aircraft, visited the met officer at Ouagadougou airport to check the forecast for the next couple of days and worked out my flight plan. The flight should take just over fifty minutes, so there was time for lunch before setting off. At half-past two, with the clouds building overhead, I taxied to the end of the runway, took off into the lumpy afternoon sky and, at two and a half thousand feet, set course for Piéla. Fifty minutes later, I tipped the aircraft on its side and looked down. Five bright tin roofs in a line, one significantly larger than the others, and a number of other buildings laid out in an orderly pattern betrayed the mission. Half a mile further on was a good-sized village of traditional round huts. I noticed that a small group of huts on the far edge of the village had their walls painted black and wondered why this should be. A flock of goats was grazing on an open patch of ground that looked as though it might be the airstrip, so I put the plane into a dive and zoomed along at head height to drive them off before attempting to land.

I parked the aircraft next to the windsock, which hung limply on a pole under the spreading boughs of a large flame tree that stood next to the first house in the line. As I did so, the missionary came out to meet me. His greeting was full of thanksgiving along the lines of "Praise the Lord for bringing you safely to this humble mission station among the heathen" and other similar incantations, all of which made my hackles rise. It was a full two minutes before he eventually drew breath, allowing me the opportunity to introduce myself. However, he had hardly shaken my hand before he was off again on the theme of "Thanks be to the Lord for His generosity in bringing us new friends to further the work of his mission among the misbegotten unbelievers" and I began to wonder if it was truly a good idea to entrust the healthcare of the local population to someone with such a tramline approach to everything.

I set about putting covers on the aircraft, since I was due to stay overnight and it was my habit to make sure the plane was fully protected whenever it was left out in the open, however remote and unthreatening the location might appear to be at first sight. At the same time, I also retrieved a set of thin metal spikes and a roll of sheep netting from the aircraft's storage bay and set up a battery operated electric perimeter fence to keep any intruders away from the plane. I had seen what inquisitive goats and small children could do to an aircraft, and a crowd of both had already started to surround us.

By the time I had finished my security precautions and had hauled my small rucksack and a notebook from the aircraft, the missionary had finished his divine thanks and was ready to walk with me over to the mission itself. On the way, I discovered that he and his wife had been there for five years, having moved from a mission a hundred miles further east, in the neighbouring tribal territory, where they had spent twelve years.

I had been told that there was also another missionary family based at the mission, but that they were presently absent on "home furlough," having served seven years without a break "in the Lord's service". Mrs Peterson, her husband told me proudly, was a registered nurse with seventeen years experience. She was assisted by two native girls who had received some nursing training. One was graded as a midwife and was presently away at the hospital in Ouagadougou for further specialist training.

The medical part of the mission was situated a hundred yards away from the mission houses and comprised two buildings made out of concrete blocks, with sloping tin roofs. One had massive steel doors, festooned with heavy padlocks, and looked as though it was probably a store. The other comprised two rooms with open apertures for windows and grass matting propped up on poles to prevent the burning sun from entering directly. A series of logs laid out in rows between the two buildings served as seating for those either waiting for treatment themselves or accompanying those who were.

The two rooms of the open building were of different sizes. The first one, which accounted for three quarters of the available space, was completely empty, with whitewashed, rendered walls and a bare concrete floor, where the sick were lying on grass mats that they had brought with them. The smaller room contained an old delivery table, a small bookcase attached to the wall above a formica counter, with about twenty books on its shelves, and a glass fronted, metal framed cabinet containing a selection of gruesome looking instruments. The walls of this room were tiled from the floor up to chest height and then whitewashed above that level, while the cement floor had a coat of worn and faded cardinal red paint.

All this could be seen through the open window aperture, but we did not enter. I thought at first that Mr Peterson must prefer to stand outside in the sun while he extolled the virtues of his mission and its work, but soon discovered that it was his wife who ruled the roost in the clinic and over all matters medical, while he simply concentrated on the evangelical work. There were quite a lot of people milling about, but I noticed that they kept well clear of us as we talked and seemed slightly reluctant to get too close to the missionary.

My moment of reverie was broken by the arrival of Mrs Peterson, who came striding over from her house with a distinct air of purpose about her. After the briefest of greetings, punctuated again by "Praise the Lord for bringing you here to help us in His work" and more of the now all too familiar incantations, she gave me a brief but comprehensive explanation of the mission's medical work. She told me that both she and Martha Whitman, the other missionary wife who was presently on "home furlough", were qualified nursing sisters, each with over seventeen years' medical mission service behind them. They provided primary medical care with an emphasis on paediatric ailments and maternity, besides dispensing medicines for the most prevalent of treatable tropical diseases, mostly fevers or gastric complaints. She listed, in some detail, the drugs that they used and the numbers of patients treated annually for each of the various complaints.

Listening to her litany, I became aware that there was a very restrictive morality about the mission's approach to illness and treatment. When I asked about tuberculosis and leprosy, both of which were endemic and very common in the region, I was told, in no uncertain terms, that these were products of the Devil's work and that she refused to treat them.

The same applied to venereal diseases, which, she declared, were only spread through immoral behaviour. At this point, her husband launched into a lecture on the mission's teaching of moral behaviour to all those who attended the clinic and I began to understand why the people waiting outside had kept their distance.

The sun was setting by the time we had finished our tour of the clinic, but there were still a number of people waiting patiently. Mr Peterson called out to them in the local language that the clinic was closed for the day and that they should come back tomorrow. He then led the way back to his house. As we passed the large building with the tin roof, which looked as though it was probably the mission church, I asked him if they had a strong congregation among the local people. I was amazed when he replied that only the mission staff were allowed to use the church building. Everyone else sat on the logs in front of the clinic and he preached to them there. I had noticed a small dais in front of the rows of logs, but until that moment its significance had eluded me.

"Don't the people want to come and join in with your church services?" I asked.

"We don't ask them to join us until they have accepted the Lord and been baptised in His name," the missionary replied. "Only the pure in heart can enter the house of the Lord."

"So how many do you have in your congregation?" I asked.

"When we are all here, including our own and the Whitmans' children, we have eleven," he replied.

"And how many of those are mission converts?" I enquired, trying to sound interested.

"Only two, the native nurse and the midwife," he said, almost proudly. "The Lord's work cannot be rushed."

The evening meal was served early, as it was their habit to eat just after dark. A plaque over the front door of the Petersons' house proclaimed "Early to bed and early to rise, the Lord's Work waits for no man" and gave me a flavour of what was in store. Mrs Peterson was a remarkably talented cook and placed an excellent meal on the table within half an hour. While we were waiting for it to be prepared, Mr Peterson showed me the plans of what they hoped to build and explained the economics of their grant application. I had to remind him several times that I had no authority or decision-making role but was merely there to report objectively on the service they provided, the facilities that existed and the extent to which new facilities were needed.

When Mrs Peterson rang a bell to announce the imminence of supper, her two children put in an appearance. Two boys, aged nine and eleven, they were stiffly polite and sat unmoving and attentive to their father, remaining silent until spoken to. As they were introduced, each, in turn, stood, shook my hand and then resumed his seat without a word. When the food had been put on the table, they sat with heads bowed while their father intoned a long prayer of thanksgiving, over half of which was a repetition of the incantations he had delivered on my arrival. He had no sooner finished than the eldest son embarked on another long prayer. The younger son followed suit and then it was Mrs Peterson's turn. She blessed the food, the farmers who had grown it, the market women from whom it had been bought and anything else she could think of, going on for almost five minutes. When she finally stopped, everyone looked at me. It was obvious that I, too, was supposed to contribute. I was momentarily tempted to stir the pot, but decided instead that brevity was called for.

"I give thanks for hospitality, good food and for the opportunity to meet new people," I said, expecting that now, at last, we might be allowed to start the meal. But no. Mr Peterson was off again with another long and complicated supplication. By the time he was done and we actually got to eat, the food had gone cold and was no longer appetising. I made excuses about being only a light eater, but noticed that the Peterson family all tucked in and ate with relish. I wondered, impishly, if this was because it was their sacred duty for, after all the blessings that had been heaped upon the food, to leave any would surely have been a mortal sin.

After supper it was apparently time for bed and Mrs Peterson explained that one of the adjacent bungalows was normally used by mission visitors and had been prepared for my use. By now, I was beginning to feel slightly oppressed by the atmosphere at the mission and declined the offer. I always carried a light camp bed and mosquito net in my aeroplane and would be perfectly comfortable under the wing. In any case, there was some routine servicing to be done, which I could do by torchlight while it was cool, before going to bed. Mr Peterson looked as though my refusal was an insult to his wife's hospitality, but she merely smiled and said: "Whatever suits you best. The bungalow is open and the bed is ready if you want it. It may rain in the night and you might be more comfortable under a roof."

"Thank you, but I'll be fine. I often sleep under the wing," I assured her and left them to settle down. Even before I had opened the plane's engine cowling I noticed that all the lights in the mission house had been extinguished. It was a matter of only ten minutes' work to clean the filters, top up the oil and do the other routine checks. Then I put together my camp bed and hung up the mosquito net.

While I was doing this, a man from the village sauntered over and greeted me. I replied in Mauré, the local language. When he asked what I was doing, I explained that to make the plane fly it was necessary to do some preparatory work, just like servicing a car or a lorry. I asked if he was one of the mission staff or whether he lived in the village, and offered him a cigarette. He accepted it with delight and asked: "So, you are not one of these missionaries, then?"

"I am not," I assured him. "But how do you know this?"

"You greet me and talk to me in my own tongue. You give me a cigarette and smoke with me and you have not mentioned God," came the soft, dry reply.

"But don't all the mission people speak Mauré?" I asked.

"Only the preaching man does. The others speak Gourmantche, but not many of our people can understand that."

"What about the nurse and the midwife, aren't they local ladies?"

"Ha! They speak a little Mauré, but they are not Mossi like us. They are Gouro people, from another land. They came here with the missionaries. Nobody trusts them."

"But they care for the sick people, don't they? How do they make themselves understood?" I asked.

"They keep people waiting in the hot sun and let the missionary tell his stories before they treat people. They do not care about sickness. Nobody likes them," the man said.

"Then why do people come here for treatment?" I asked.

"It is the only place. Père Dominic and the Sisters at the Catholic mission help those they can, but they are not medical people. Most of the people who go to them have been refused help here. Père Dominic has even built houses for the lepers and other outcasts."

I thought about this for a moment, realising that I was going to have to ask some difficult questions in the morning.

"Why have you come here?" the man asked quietly, breaking the brief silence as we sat there in the darkness.

"The mission has asked for money to build a new maternity and dispensary building," I told him.

"Give it to the Catholics on the other side of the village. They are kind people," he said instantly, with a snort of what sounded like disgust.

"Will you be here tomorrow?" I inquired. "I should like to meet you again before I go."

"Can you help a sick child that these people have refused?" he asked, ignoring my question.

"I will try," I assured him. "If necessary, I could take the child and a parent back with me to Ouagadougou to the big hospital."

"I will come in the morning," he said, rising abruptly.

Before he left, I gave him the rest of the packet of cigarettes and some matches and he pressed a *kola* nut into my palm. I settled down on my camp bed with a lot to think about and was lulled to sleep by the buzz of nocturnal insects.

I was woken by raised voices and a long drawn out wailing sound. There were lamps coming and going between the various mission buildings and it was obvious that something was happening. I guessed that one of the heavily pregnant women I had noticed hanging about the place in the afternoon was about to give birth and decided to go and see the mission's medical service in action. I kept a good bright torch in the plane, so I took this with me and headed over towards the source of all the wailing.

The maternity unit appeared to be a hive of activity, with a lot of anxious women crowding round the open window of the smaller room. I joined the crowd and asked what was going on. Someone told me that a girl was trying to deliver her baby, but that there were complications.

"Isn't there another midwife here?" I asked, and the women all laughed.

"The only one there was has left," they told me. "She has gone home to Bobo-Dioulasso."

"Mr Peterson told me she had gone to Ouagadougou for special training," I said and they laughed even more derisively.

"She told us there was too much God for her to be able to work here. She has gone home," the woman insisted.

"Mrs Peterson is an experienced nurse," I said. "Surely she can deliver the baby."

"She is too busy praying," said one women, and another added: "She cannot even speak our language, how can she help? She cannot speak to the mother."

"You speak our language," said someone else. "You are surely a doctor. Can you not help?"

"I'm not a doctor," I explained. But at least I could talk to the mother, I thought, and find out what the problem was. I pushed my way through the press of bodies and was almost squirted into the room. A girl of only fifteen or sixteen was lying on the delivery table, writhing and screaming in pain. Two older women, who turned out to be her mother and her aunt, were trying to calm and soothe her without much success. Mrs Peterson was on her knees in the corner, oblivious to all the commotion, muttering prayers like there was no tomorrow.

I asked the girl's mother what the problem was and she explained that this was her daughter's first child and that it was breach. A midwife was needed to turn it round, so that it could come out properly. She was very afraid for her daughter. I turned to Mrs Peterson and asked what she was going to do to help. She ignored me. I put my hand on her shoulder to try and get her attention, but she just brushed me off and continued with her incantations, oblivious to everything around her and her eyes tightly shut. I took hold of her shoulder and shook her, shouting loudly in her ear, but got no more response. She was clearly in the throes of some sort of breakdown and was of no use at all in the present emergency. However, somebody had to do something – and quickly.

Another agonised scream from the girl on the table galvanised me. Remembering the books that I had noticed when I visited the room earlier, I rushed to the bookcase, which was locked. I broke it open and scanned the titles. Among the dog-eared volumes was an old Belgian obstetrics text book, dating from 1936 and featuring a lot of detailed diagrams and drawings. Better than nothing, I thought, flicking through the pages. It didn't take long to find a section that dealt with the present situation. Some instruments and supplies would be needed and I also needed to wash my hands. I asked the faces in the window if someone would boil some water and was assured that it was already being done and would be ready soon. I had forgotten that birth in rural Africa is a communal event and felt reassured that there was a lot of wisdom and assistance all around me when it was needed.

The instrument cupboard was also locked and there was no sign of the key. Desperate times need desperate measures, so I used the heel of my torch and cracked the glass, selecting what looked to be the most useful instruments from the shelves and dropping them into a stainless steel dish. I found a bottle of disinfectant and a jar of what I hoped was grease, together with some sutures in glass vials. These were put on the counter top.

The boiling water was ready by then, so some of it went in the dish with the instruments and a splash of disinfectant and a bit more went into a bowl for me to wash in. I called for more lights, and a number of lanterns were passed through the window and hung from the rafters. With the aunt holding my bright torch and someone else holding the obstetrics book at my elbow, I took a deep breath and started work.

One learns some odd and unusual skills when living and working in the African bush, but this was definitely a new one. How the girl and her infant survived I have no idea, but two hours later, as I was tying off the last suture, the mother was feeding her new-born daughter and neither seemed too much the worse for wear. With my hand liberally coated with whatever was in the pot I thought was grease, I had pushed and twisted, pulled and turned. Using a scalpel, I had then cut deep to make the birth canal larger and finally the baby had emerged. I held my breath in dread while the grandmother held it aloft by its feet and smacked it smartly on its scrawny bottom.

Apart from the mutterings of Mrs Peterson that still came from the corner of the room, there was a long silence. All the women looking through the open window and the doorway were holding their breath, just like me. There was a hesitant sucking sound and then that magical moment when the baby let out a lusty yell and we were all able to breathe freely again. The other women were more than competent to deal with the afterbirth and cleaning up the new mother. Within half an hour she was on her feet, with her baby suckling well.

The delivery room was now empty apart from the missionary's wife, who was still on her knees in the corner. After cleaning the place up, I went outside and sat on a log to talk with all the women who had attended the birth. They were a happy bunch, delighted to chatter and offering me bits of fruit, toasted corn cobs and a calabash of cool water.

We talked until sunrise, and it was then that Mr Peterson arrived on the scene. He seemed surprised to discover me there and even more so to find me in the middle of a vigorous and good humoured discussion with the local women. The previous afternoon he had described these same people as surly – and their manner certainly changed as soon as he approached. It didn't take long for me to understand why. He asked what was going on and I told him there had been a birth during the night and that I was just chatting to some of the new mother's friends and relatives. He asked about the baby and who the mother was.

"The child is a little girl," I told him. "The mother is called Alaoumye and she is sixteen and a half years old. This is her first child."

"Where is my wife?" he asked.

"Still inside, praying," I said and he looked a little puzzled.

"She's been there all night," I continued.

"But she delivered...."

"No, she didn't deliver the baby. But it's fine – although the mother could do with a course of antibiotics to make sure she doesn't get an infection. I think you should encourage your wife to go home now."

He went and looked in through the window, calling to his wife. She ignored him. After three attempts, he went round behind the building, where there was a well, and returned with a bucket of water. He strode into the room and poured the whole bucket over his wife's head before retiring smartly. His wife let out a howl of protest and came storming out of the maternity unit screaming at the local women for being heathen savages who did not deserve the Lord's bounty or His love. I noticed that Mr Peterson was no longer in evidence and did nothing to own up to having drenched his wife. After a few moments of outraged comments, she strode off in the direction of her own house and I decided that this might be an opportune moment to explore the village.

There, I soon encountered the man who had stopped to talk to me the previous night and I received a very friendly greeting. He asked me again about helping the child he had spoken of. It was his brother's son, he explained, but his brother had contracted TB and the missionaries at the clinic had refused to treat him or any of his family. His brother had now died and his son needed help; would I look at him? I explained, again, that I was not a doctor, but he said that since I had delivered Alaoumye's baby I must be able to help. He gestured to a woman behind him to come forward and show me her child.

Malnutrition is very obvious and this poor little boy was like a skeleton. I asked the man to take me to Père Dominic's house and together we walked through to the far side of the village. The old priest must have been in his seventies, but was still vigorous and friendly. He called one of the two nuns who lived nearby, saying Sister Juliette would certainly know what to do. The nun took one look at the baby and at his mother and said simply: "They both need food. Come." Taking the baby, she then walked off, leaving the mother to follow.

Père Dominic invited me and my new friend to have breakfast with him and we walked back together to his house. He had already heard about the night's events and remarked that it was fortunate there was a visiting doctor. I had to explain once more that I was not a doctor and I told him what the purpose of my visit was. He asked about Mrs Peterson, having also been told about her prayer vigil.

"The poor woman is afraid of these people because she has not learned their tongue," he said with a slightly sad tone. "She spent many years among the Gourmantche people and speaks their language, but after almost five years here she has learned nothing. Maybe it would be better if she went back to Canada. We seldom meet and we can offer little help since their religious style and doctrine are alien to us and they will not speak to us. Even so, I will pray for her."

I left him soon after that, giving him a large denomination note to pay for feeding the little boy and his mother.

"That will feed fifty for several months," he protested.

"I'm sure you will use it wisely," I said, thanking him for breakfast and setting off to walk back through the village.

The Protestant mission was a hive of activity when I arrived. I was soon surrounded by chattering people, all wanting to talk about the night's events and at the same time waiting for the dispensary to open so that their own ills could be treated. They told me that they would have to sit through a long sermon from Mr Peterson before that happened, but if they didn't stay to listen there would be no medicine.

At half-past eight Mr Peterson came across from his house, clutching a bible in his hand. His wife was one pace behind, dressed in a starched white nursing uniform and looking tense and nervous. The missionary explained that it was their custom to have a short prayer meeting before opening the clinic and asked what time I intended to leave.

"You know my brief, Mr Peterson. I need to see the clinic in action, to discuss the treatments it offers, the staff and equipment and the project that has been proposed. Then I have to get back and write a report about it. I do not need to concern myself with your mission and these good people have already been waiting several hours for the clinic to open. Perhaps we should begin with the treatment and then I can be on my way before noon?"

" But the people expect prayers before the clinic…," he started to protest.

"And by the sound of them, they don't appreciate it or pay much attention, do they?" I interrupted. "Perhaps they might show a bit more interest if they felt that the treatment was less conditional. Now, I am going over to my aircraft to get my notebook. When I come back I should like to see the clinic at work, if you please." With that I left him and headed across the two hundred yards that lay between the clinic and my plane. Not giving him much option, I retrieved my notebook, replaced my torch in its bracket and turned back towards the mission.

Mr Peterson was already on his podium and in full flow. He looked slightly flustered and dribbled to a stop as I arrived back in front of the clinic. His wife then unlocked the dispensary door and opened the steel shutter over the window as the first patient shuffled forward. I went over and leaned on the open window sill to watch and listen, occasionally talking to the patients when Mrs Peterson's lack of language became a problem. Many of the patients were there for repeat doses of mundane medicaments and there were few new cases that needed diagnostic enquiries.

When Alaoumye presented herself, I thought Mrs Peterson was going to have a fit as she tried to chase her out. That was the point at which I intervened. I went inside and insisted that she give the girl a good antibiotic to prevent any risk of infection. I was well aware that the night's procedure, if one dared call it that, had been far from sterile and that infection was a far greater risk than it would have been had the delivery been normal. Reluctantly, she counted out three capsules.

"That will only be enough for today," I said. "What about the rest of the course?"

"If I give them all to her now she will simply hand the rest out to other women and the treatment will be wasted," she insisted. It was obvious that she did not trust her patients to take their medicines responsibly and had a very low opinion of the Mossi women.

I talked to Alaoumye for a few moments and assured myself that she understood how to take the drugs and why it was important to take the full course in the right way. She repeated back the instructions with no problem. She had a baby to protect and I felt sure she would do it right.

"Well, I suggest you trust this girl," I told Mrs Peterson. "I have the impression you might be happier not having to see her every day after last night. You'll still be doing the Lord's work by giving her all the medicine now."

With very bad grace, she counted out the capsules and put them in a bottle. I picked it up and handed it to the girl, who smiled and thanked me. She was about to leave when she turned back and asked me my name.

"Ian," I said, and she repeated it. Nodding her thanks, she gave me a lovely smile and walked out into the sunlight.

After another half an hour I had seen and heard enough. I thanked Mrs Peterson for her hospitality and said I would get my report off to the NGO within a couple of days. Her husband was waiting for me outside, looking rather grey and very worried. As I also thanked him for his hospitality and an eventful visit, he asked if I could tell him how I would report on his project.

"Oh, I shall report positively," I told him. "There is a clear need for a good medical facility in this region and it would be sensible to build on what already exists. However, I shall propose some conditions on the grant." I watched his worry increase as I said this.

"What sort of conditions?" he enquired tentatively.

"Well, I do feel you need more people who speak Mauré, since that is the language of the people you work with. It is all very well you having some command of the language, but you are a preacher and not involved in the medical work. You must have medical staff who can talk to the patients, especially when your local nurses are not here to assist. There may be some other recommendations, but let me work it out first. I will send you a copy of my report, so you will know exactly what is said."

He looked slightly relieved by this, but clearly still had some worries. "Why didn't you say that it was you who delivered that baby last night?" he asked.

"Would it change anything?" I asked.

"What do you mean?"

"Well, sometimes you may get a better response by acting first and hoping that your actions will lead people to see your point of view. That girl would have died if somebody had not done something. As it is, she and her baby are alive and have at least the same chance of remaining that way as other new mothers and their babies. I am sure your wife now understands that."

We had now reached the plane and as I took the covers off and rolled up the goat fence, Mr Peterson seemed lost in thought. With everything stowed and my external checks done, I walked over to say goodbye. As he shook my hand he began one of his vigorous "Praise the Lord" blessings and I felt obliged to stop him.

"Please don't," I said. "Some years ago the Royal Air Force spent the best part of two million pounds teaching me to fly and to take care of my aircraft. I would prefer to place my trust in that training and my knowledge of the African bush. If I have not done my job properly, perhaps I do not deserve any divine assistance." I climbed in, did up my straps, ran through the cockpit checks and started the engine." Mr Peterson looked somewhat dejected as I taxied to the end of the strip, where I brought the aircraft to a halt in order to run through the final checks before take-off.

Standing beside the runway was Père Dominic, holding a bunch of letters. Opening the door, I beckoned him over and asked if he would like me to post them for him. He seemed pleased and as he handed them over asked: "How do you spell your name?"

It seemed an odd question, but I told him and then asked why he wanted to know.

"Because Alaoumye has been to see me. She wants me to baptise her new daughter. She has given her your name and I need to know how to record it," he said, waving me away.

I reached into the bag behind my seat and produced the two bottles of red wine that I had somewhat misguidedly brought with me and handed them to him. "Perhaps you and the good Sisters could find a good use for these," I said. "I don't think the Petersons would have accepted them."

"Thank you," he replied with a conspiratorial grin. "One I will bless and we will use it for communion wine. The other we will save and drink on the day of our mission's patron, St Francis."

He closed the cabin door. I opened the throttle and rumbled down the dirt runway, waving to Mr Peterson as I passed and took off wondering what he would think of a girl named Ian.

Glossary

A number of African words have been included in the text because there is no direct or appropriate English equivalent. Such words have been italicized and the following notes will clarify their meanings:

calabash: A type of gourd, the skin of which is dried and then used as a bowl or bottle. *(see Footprints In The Dust)*

doki-boy: A groom or ostler. Doki is the Hausa word for a horse, so literally a 'horse boy'. *(see Footprints In The Dust)*

dolo: This is the Mauré name for a village beer made from fermented millet and sorghum grains. It is most commonly a milky grey colour, like thick barley water, and often has fragments of husk and straw floating in it. The colour may vary according to the water and the type of grain used, but the starch sludge that floats in suspension is an important part of the beverage. Often with a slightly sour taste, it can have quite a high alcohol content and pack a punch as good as any strong ale in Britain. It is generally drunk from a calabash (qv), which is passed round from person to person and swirled by tilting the bowl to mix up the sludge before drinking. *(see San Prison Blues and Bones of Contention)*

fou-fou: This is the name used across much of Africa for the starch that forms the staple diet. It is generally a smooth, porridge-like paste made from any one of a variety of different tubers, including yams, cassava (manioc), taro, sweet potato or g'ubani, an insignificant looking forest plant which produces a single large swollen root about two feet below the ground surface.

In each case the tubers are peeled, washed, boiled and then mashed in a large wooden mortar with a log sized pestle. In some areas they are grated after the first cooking to make the mashing easier. The resultant pulp is then steamed until the texture is just right. Fou-fou is eaten with the fingers together with a wide variety of sauces, stews – when meat or stockfish is available – and vegetables which are usually either spiced or loaded with hot peppers. *(see The Missionary's Feet)*

gaabi: This is a coarse cotton cloak worn by the Afar people of the Danakil, along with many others in Ethiopia. It is made up of several layers of fabric and sometimes has a coloured edge. The edge is purely decorative and its colour has no significance among the Afar. *(see The Man of Passage)*

g'ubani: is the edible root of a species of ground vine that bears fruits which are poisonous to man. Like some varieties of bitter manioc (cassava), the tuber contains a low concentration of cyanide which requires extensive washing during preparation. The taste is nutty and the fou-fou that it produces (see above) tends to be slightly gritty. *(see A Short Walk In Ituri)*

gurri: The Wa-Wa man had a collection of bones that he would cast on an antelope skin as part of the divination process for diagnosing illness, when concocting traditional medicines or for forecasting future events such as rain, harvests or childbirth. Accompanied by esoteric incantations and chants, the bones are cast according to an ancient and secret ritual, known only to the initiates of his craft, and their position and distribution has great significance. The bones themselves are important, each having a special significance and magical properties of its own. The gurri was one of these bones and had originally been the top vertebra from the neck of our witch doctor's grandfather, who had himself been a noted sorcerer. *(see Bones of Contention)*

inayenyii: This was another of the Wa-wa man's treasured bones. It was said to have been one of his paternal grandmother's ribs. This woman had been a noted sorceress of whom people still spoke with awe and great respect. *(see Bones of Contention)*

ingwane bushes: These shoulder-high forest bushes produce foliage similar to the shinga'a leaves (qv) I had known in the West African savanna. I learned their name from the women who redressed my injured arm in the forest village. *(see A Short Walk In Ituri)*

kola nut: A two-lobed nut-like fruit that is chewed for its mild narcotic effect. Usually pink, it stains the gums, tongue and teeth bright red. *(see Sankarani)*

malafou or **malafu:** This is another of the locally produced alcoholic beverages and is made from palm sap. Similar recipes exist across Africa, with many different names. Malafu is made by collecting the fresh sap of the oil palm in a bottle that is then lightly stoppered with a twist of grass and left in the sun for most of the day to ferment. It is generally a milky white colour, very slightly oily, with an aroma of sour coconut. It also has a kick like a mule! In some places, the brew is filtered through charcoal in a closely woven basket and then kept in a shady place for several days to develop its potency. This was the sort of malafu most commonly made in Amézodjikopé when Arnie Slomann first arrived. He later adapted the process to produce some truly remarkable palm wines. *(see Arnie's Wives)*

mongongo leaves: Many forest leaves are quite large, although most of the best ones are found high up in the canopy. Mongongo was the name given by the BaMbuti people I met in Ituri to the leaves they used to thatch their huts. They are spade shaped, about 50 or 60 cm long and 30 to 40 cm wide, with thick stems. The upper surface is very glossy and the leaves are quite stiff, so laid like overlapping scales, with the stalks woven into the hut's frame, they make ideal roofing material. In the humid environment of the forest, they seldom need replacing before the people move camp and build new huts. *(see A Short Walk In Ituri)*

mundele ya barba: This was the Lingala term used to describe any bearded foreigner. It means literally 'white man with a beard' and was repeated many times, almost like a chant, by village children in communities I visited throughout the northern part of Zaïre. *(see Hippopotamus Hiatus)*

niseke: A term used to describe a whole range of complex ideas and beliefs relating to those who have contact with the spirit world or who demonstrate abilities, skills and qualities beyond the normal comprehension of ordinary people. Whilst mostly used as a term of respect and admiration it can also be one of suspicion, apprehension or awe. *(see Hippopotamus Hiatus)*

shinga'a leaves: The African bush has many shrubs and trees that bear glossy leaves. Some are still almost unknown to western botanists and thus have only their local names. Some of these leaves have a particularly waxy surface and are large and pliable, remaining fresh for several days after they have been picked. This makes them ideal for wrapping food to take when travelling or working in fields some distance from the village. Shinga'a was the local name for such a plant in the area where the Sankarani River lies.

The leaves look similar to those of laurel but are larger, measuring about 30 cm long by 12 cm wide, and are of a slightly softer texture. The word shinga is also used locally to described clothing that is wrapped around the body. *(see Sankarani)*

wiwe bark: The bark of many trees can be peeled off in long strips and used as bowstrings or for binding things together in the same way that rattan is used in the Far East, or raffia where palm trees grow. Wiwe was the local name in Western Mali for one such variety of bark. *(see Sankarani)*

Waziri: the Emir's principal counsellor or Prime Minister, also known as a Vizier or Wazir in other Muslim cultures. *(see Footprints In The Dust)*

Acknowledgements

Many people contribute to the writing, design and publication of a book like this, from those who participated in the events that I have recounted right through to those who have helped to bring the stories to the printed page. Most of them, inevitably, remain anonymous, but I do recognise their contributions none the less and I am most grateful for them.

Special thanks must go to my editors, Jill Todd and Mike Cable, for their patience with my sometimes quirky writing style, their hard work, expert advice, attention to detail and enthusiastic encouragement from beginning to end.

In remote corners of Africa, there were so many people who made me welcome and allowed me to share their lives and cultures, not just as an onlooker, but as an involved participant and friend. Sadly, with the passage of time and the often all-too-short life expectancy of rural Africa, many of them are no longer around, but my memories and appreciation of them remain clear and enduring.

To all those friends and other unnamed individuals who have read parts of the text and offered opinions, constructive comments, criticism, support and encouragement – many thanks. Your input has been extremely helpful, immensely valuable and much appreciated.

Most of all, I am indebted to my wife, Gay, not just for her unfailing support, robust criticism and mastery of words, from which I have learned enormously, but also for her infinite patience. Without Gay's contribution this book might never have appeared in print.

The Drawings

Masks of the type depicted here and elsewhere in the book represent an integral part of tribal culture in many countries throughout Africa. These line drawings were made by the author during the years he spent living and working among the various communities, sketched either from life or from photographs that he took at the time.

Senufo initiation mask,
Côte d'Ivoire

Dan mask, Côte d'Ivoire

Akua fertility doll,
Ashanti, Ghana

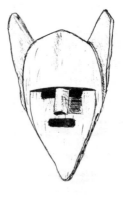

Bambara dancing mask

Baulé, brass mask,
Guinée

Ewe dancing mask,
Togo

Basonghe dancing
mask, Zaïre

Senufo initiation mask,
Côte d'Ivoire

Ibo mask, S. E. Nigeria

Bambara crocodile
dancing mask, Mali

229

Bakongo, Zaïre

BaPende dancing
Mask, Guinée

BaPende ritual mask,
Zaïre

Guro mask, Côte d'Ivoire

BaLuba mask, Zaïre

Bushongo dancing
mask, Zaïre

Baulé, Côte d'Ivoire/Guinée

Other books by the same author

Keep Taking the Pills is an anthology of verse from the Transplant Ward. After a successful kidney transplant in 2000, Ian found himself back in hospital for an extended stay with another problem. The sufferings of a fellow transplantee prompted a silly verse and one thing then led to another. As a result, the walls of the ward were soon papered with odes generated to relieve the tedium of hospital routine. Together with some inspired cartoons, these poems were brought together in this anthology to be sold for the benefit of other kidney patients.

Keep Taking the Pills was published in 2002 by Ducketts Press.
ISBN 0-9542844-0-2

Available from:
GTPR Ltd
1 Dog Lane, Fenny Compton
Southam CV47 2YD

Telephone: 01295 770207
Fax: 01295 770202
Email: books@gtpr.com

Forthcoming titles

Bride Price. Sent to the tropical jungle of central Africa to teach villagers how to develop clean drinking water supplies, Ian lived for some time in a village deep in the forest. While he was there, the village elders and a witch doctor, together with the local political agent, persuaded him to foster Abélé, an orphan from the community who had been ostracised because her parents, who had died in an epidemic, were considered niseke. In many tribal societies, girls marry young, and men still pay a bride price for their wives. So, when an undesirable suitor asked for Abélé as his wife, Ian faced a major dilemma. This is the compelling tale of how he eventually managed to solve this complex problem by carefully and rather ingeniously negotiating his way through the minefield of local customs, taboos and traditions while at the same time having to deal with fierce intrigue and even cannibalistic violence.

Due for publication in 2007.

Ambakwaka is a collection of traditional West African folk tales featuring that likeable rogue and trickster called Kwaku Ananse. He appears in many cultures and is sometimes also known as The Spider. These tales, passed down by generations of story tellers, would be told at night in the villages, around flickering fires. They serve both as moral tales and as a ritualised form of entertainment.